The high road has less traffic™

honest advice on the path
through love and divorce

MONIQUE A. HONAMAN

The high road has less traffic™

"Monique writes as if she is sitting in the family room of her home sharing conversation with a friend over a cup of coffee. As she unfolds the story of her journey from marriage to divorce to re-marriage, the reader is able to experience with her the pains, fears, doubts, tears, and frustrations, and then her emergence into forgiveness that opens the way for her to walk the high road into a new life. This is a phenomenal read that will help bring healing for those wounded from divorce. I could not put it down."

— Dr. D. B. Shelnutt, Jr.

"Monique NAILED IT! I highly recommend this book to any woman going through a divorce (and to her friends!). Monique gives a very honest, real and practical view on divorce and the 'bottom line.' There are many roads we can choose to take but in reality the ONLY choice we must make for ourselves and our children (and yes! even our ex-) is the 'high road.' As Monique points out, moving forward with integrity is paramount to being able to move forward. As someone who took the 'high road,' the rewards and peace of mind and heart are endless"

— SLB (recently divorced mother)

"Monique's book is an excellent resource for parents experiencing divorce. Through her own passionate and candid story, Monique provides common sense advice from a sound psychological perspective that will help women dealing with the pain and challenges of divorce. Humor is combined with hard facts to provide survival skills for the affected spouse and healing for the whole family."

— Dr. Marcia H. Rogers, Psy.D.
Licensed Psychologist, Divorce Care for Children (DC4K) Leader

"This is a must-read book for any woman facing divorce. Monique was brutally honest and painfully open about her situation while bringing hope, laughter, faith, and belief to what seems like a devastating life-event. Her advice to always 'take the high road' is truly what it's all about."

— MLA (recently divorced mom of 2)

For Kendall and Harrison, my amazing children,
for inspiring me to take the high road each and every day!
I love you both more than you will ever know.

For my mom and my brother
for being there for me and my kids in so many ways.

For all of my wonderful friends who surrounded me with love during
my darkest of days … especially Ann, Kathleen, Stacy and Ellen.

For Pastor Dee … for your prayers, wisdom and counsel.

For Justin … for encouraging me to "Let Go and Let God,"
for reminding me that "God Has a Plan,"
and for showing me that "All Things are Possible."

I love you all. xo-moho

About The Author

Within weeks of being told, "I don't love you and I want a divorce," Monique A. Honaman promised herself, "I won't go through this agonizing event without turning it around and helping others to learn from it." In *The High Road Has Less Traffic*, Monique shares her personal journey, prepares you for the unexpected hazards, and explains the realization that taking the "high road" can be the most self-fulfilling and productive "exit strategy" to follow for the good of all involved, especially children. In this altogether humorous, inspirational and always poignant survival guide, Monique tackles parenthood and adultery, self-image and social networking, old girlfriends and new boy "friends," and the rediscovered joy of family and forgiveness. Take it straight from the heart. *The High Road Has Less Traffic* is soul food to go!

Monique lives in suburban Atlanta with her husband, Justin, and her two children. Free time is devoted to family activities like cheering for her kids at their sporting events, golfing, boating, traveling, taking photographs, reading, and volunteering in the community. Monique is also the Founder and President of ISHR Group which provides global solutions in the area of leadership assessment, development and coaching. She holds a Bachelors Degree from the University of Michigan, a Masters Degree from Michigan State University, and a Juris Doctorate from Albany Law School. Monique loves to write and is a frequent contributor to business periodicals on the subject of leadership and coaching.

In the spirit of giving back, a portion of the proceeds from sales of this book will be donated to organizations that support helping women and children transition through divorce as seamlessly as possible.

For more information, please visit: **www.HighRoadLessTraffic.com**.

"That was rough.... Thing to do now is try and forget it.... I guess I don't quite mean that. It's not a thing you can forget. Maybe not even a thing you want to forget... Life's like that sometimes... Now and then for no good reason a man can figure out, life will just haul off and knock him flat, slam him again' the ground so hard it seems like all his insides is busted. But it's not all like that. A lot of it's mighty fine, and you can't afford to waste the good part frettin' about the bad. That makes it all bad... Sure, I know – sayin' it's one thing and feelin' it's another. But I'll tell you a trick that's sometimes a big help. When you start lookin' around for something good to take the place of the bad, as a general rule you can find it."

~ From the movie *Old Yeller*

Table of Contents

Life 7

Looking Back on it All: The Prologue. 8

1   Hearing the News: The Pronouncement .12

2   Discovering the Midlife Crisis:
Just Buy a Red Convertible and Be Done With It! 15

3   Giving Your Best to Your Spouse:
Show Love and Respect Every Single Day!. 24

4   Taking the High Road:
It is ALL About the Best Interests of Your Children 32

5   Getting the Word Out: Why is Telling Mom so Tough? 38

6   Telling the Kids:
The Most Difficult Thing You Will Ever Have to Do 43

7   Putting your Plan Together: Things to Think About 53

8   Figuring it Out: 'Social Networking' Has a Whole New Meaning . . .60

9   Interpreting the Signs: Should I be Worried?. 67

10 Leaning on your Support Network: Friends and Many Others!. 74

11 Managing your Vices: Skinny and Sad, or Fat and Happy? 82

12 Using The "F" Word: The Power of Forgiveness. 85

13 Partnering with an Attorney: You Can't Do This on Your Own 91

14 Celebrating 40: Will I Ever Have Sex Again? 99

15 Being There for Your Friends: It's a Two-Way Street. 104

16 Taking Pride in New Accomplishments: I Conquered the Grill! . . .109

17 Spending Time Alone: Learn to Relish and Recharge 112

18 Saying Thank You: You're at 100%. 115

19 Becoming Friends: We'll be Like Bruce and Demi. 119

20 Moving Forward: Imagine the Possibilities 123

21 Enjoying God's Sense of Humor: A Date, Seriously? 129

22 Introducing "Friends" to your Kids:
Laying the Proper Foundation 133

23 Looking Back on it All: The Epilogue. 137

24 My Final Bottom Line. 140

A good friend gave this to me several years ago and I found it provided great hope and inspiration! Enjoy ...

Life

The most useless thing to do ... worry.

The greatest joy ... giving.

The greatest loss ... self-respect.

The most satisfying work ... helping others.

The ugliest personality trait ... selfishness.

The most endangered species ... dedicated leaders.

Our greatest natural resource ... our youth.

The greatest "shot in the arm" ... encouragement.

The greatest problem to overcome ... fear.

The most effective sleeping aid ... peace of mind.

The most powerful force in life ... love.

The most dangerous pariah ... a gossiper.

The world's most incredible computer ... the brain.

The worst thing to be without ... hope.

The deadliest weapon ... the tongue.

The two most power-filled words ... I can.

The greatest asset ... earth.

The most worthless emotion ... self-pity.

The most prized possession ... integrity.

The most beautiful attire ... a smile.

The most powerful channel of communication ... prayer.

The most contagious spirit ... enthusiasm.

The most important thing in life ... God.

PROLOGUE:
LOOKING BACK ON IT ALL

"We have no right to
ask when sorrow comes,
'Why did this happen to me?'
unless we ask the same
question for every moment
of happiness that
comes our way."

~ Anonymous

It was NEVER going to be me. Never in a million years did I ever think that I would become the 40-year old divorcee, the single mom, the "one whose husband left her." Not that anyone gets married thinking that they will end up divorced, but I "knew" it would never be me. Seriously. Never. And then, life happened!

I was blind sided when it happened to me. People asked me, "Didn't you see this coming. Didn't you have a clue?" At that point, not at all! Hindsight is 20/20, so in retrospect I see that my husband had begun to check out over the past few years, but the night that he made "The Pronouncement" I felt completely blind sided. I didn't see the clues. I felt like I had been sucker-punched in the gut. Literally. And, it took my breath away.

I like to read. As my situation unraveled, I began searching for books that would explain my situation, that would help me survive, that would provide some answers. There are some great books out there, but what I really needed more than anything, was practical, no-nonsense, light-hearted advice. My goal in writing this book is to provide just that: the tips, the advice, the listening ear that make going through this situation just a little more manageable. I needed the girlfriend who was going to give it to me straight-up, not watered down, and make me laugh, and help me contemplate my future, even when I didn't think I had it in me.

Divorce is a horrible thing. It's horrible for all involved. The husband and wife who once pledged true love. The extended family. The children. The friends (his, mine, ours). But, divorce continues to be a reality. Statistics don't lie.

In 2005, there were over 2 million marriages in the US. The marriage rate was 7.5 (per 1000 people). The divorce rate was 3.6 (per 1000 people). That's right ... more than half of all marriages end in divorce. What an ugly statistic! Always a bright side, the divorce rate is actually declining (as is the marriage rate). The divorce rate in 2005 was the lowest it had been since 1970. It was down from 4.2 in 2000, and 4.7 is 1990. The peak was at 5.3 in 1981. (Sources: U.S. Census Bureau, National Center for Health Statistics).

Life is so serious as it is. Divorce is a serious reality. This book is about sharing what I went through in hopes of helping others get through what is typically a most difficult and challenging time. My goal for this book is to provide the hug, the advice and a few smiles to what is a life-changing situation. I'm hoping to make this a bit more tolerable, and more importantly, to give some sound advice and give women (and frankly, the friends who are supporting them through this) a few things to think about in the process.

I am not writing this to share the details of what happened between my ex-husband and me. What's done is done and we've both moved on. I am writing this because since my husband told me he was leaving me I have become a magnet for other women going through the same thing. It's amazing, and sad, to me to count how many women have come to me for advice and counsel. Sharing my story, what I've learned, and the way my kids and I have dealt with this has apparently proved to be helpful to others. If I can make the process of divorce easier on just one person, one child, one family, then this project is all worthwhile.

I also need to say that my ex-husband and I are now "friends." I have completely and fully forgiven him. Not to make this all "sunshine and roses," but we are capable of having a productive conversation. We don't have dinner together. We don't vacation with our children together. But, we are capable of being at the same sporting event or school event without making everyone else feel uncomfortable. We have coffee together about once a quarter to make sure we stay on the same page with respect to our kids. I didn't ever believe that would be possible when we were in the midst of our divorce. Actually, I didn't ever want that to be possible.

Then the reality of the situation hit me. This man is the father of my children. He is going to be in my life for the rest of my life. High-School graduation. College graduation. Weddings. Grand-kids. I've just aged my children (and myself) beyond comprehension, but that is reality. I can't stress enough the need to be civil for the sake of our children. That has been my guiding principle, my high road, throughout this entire ordeal, and will continue to guide my decisions.

This is not a faith-based book, but my faith is a strong part of who I am, and you will find several references to my faith, to my beliefs and to the power of prayer. I have spoken with women who are Christian, women who are Jewish, women who are Islamic and women who have never really acknowledged a strong practicing faith, and they all recognized turning to a higher power, to God in however they define Him, during the tumultuous times of divorce.

I know some people judged me and our situation initially. I think there was an assumption that if I was such a good Christian woman that this wouldn't be happening to me. To all of that, I say bull! Divorce happens to anyone and everyone regardless of their gender, ethnicity, age, social status or religious beliefs. I subscribe to the notion of marriage as a covenant made before God to be taken very seriously. I know God wants a husband and a wife to be married. But, I also subscribe to the Ten Commandments.

Proceeding with the divorce process wasn't easy for me. I knew I would have to be able to look myself and my kids in the eyes in the future and be able to confidently say, with every ounce of sincerity, that I did all I could to save our marriage. And, I do feel I can say that – wholeheartedly. I did all I could, but unfortunately, it takes two to make a marriage work. Some people ask whether I should have been more patient and waited for my ex-husband to "come around" and "get over his midlife crisis." That would never have worked for me.

I know I did all I could to validate that my marriage was indeed over, and once I felt 100% convicted in that belief, once I knew that there wasn't a .00000001% chance that we would be able to make it work, then I resolved in my heart to get through this divorce with as much dignity, poise, and integrity that I could. I want my kids to look back on this situation and think, "WOW MOM!" I want them to know that the decisions I made were with their best interests at heart.

Divorce sucks. Being lied to sucks. Seeing your children get hurt really, really sucks. But, if you look at the statistics, divorce continues to be a reality. Very early on in this journey I knew that I wouldn't go through this, that I couldn't go through this, without learning more about who I am and becoming a better person, and without doing something to help other women in similar situations.

This is my story. We all have a story. My hope is that the advice provided in this book will apply to any person going through a divorce, for whatever reason. I've told my story countless times. It's frightening how many similarities there are with the stories I hear from other women. And, of course, there are always the differences. I've been told I have some valuable perspectives to offer. I have already been a listening ear, offering snippets of advice to so many women going through similar situations. I've been amazed by their strength, their resiliency, their faith, and their sense of humor. Oprah Winfrey once said, "Turn your wounds into wisdom." I had many wounds that I'm hoping I can turn into wisdom to share with you.

I leave every encounter with other women going through the same thing feeling as though this is my mission. I want to help others get through this, and not just survive, but thrive. I want to help other women from looking back and saying, "How could I have been so stupid?" I want to let you know that you are not alone in this. Other women, lots of them unfortunately, have traveled this road before you. And, let me tell you, the high road has less traffic!

HEARING THE NEWS:
THE PRONOUNCEMENT

*"I now pronounce you
husband and wife ...
for richer, for poorer,
in sickness and health,
through good times
and bad ..."*

Like most married couples, we were "pronounced" husband and wife when we married in May 1992. "The Pronouncement" came to carry an entirely different meaning 16 years later.

Father's Day. How ironic is that? My ex- and I had spent a long weekend at the lake with extended family. He had moved to Denver for a new job seven months earlier. The kids (our daughter was nine years old, our son was seven) and I had stayed behind in Atlanta waiting for our house to sell before we moved west to join him. This was our weekend to say goodbye to my family. We were moving to Colorado in five weeks. My mom and her husband came in from South Carolina. My brother, his wife and their two kids, drove down from Ohio. We spent the weekend enjoying each other's company since we weren't sure when we would all be together again.

It was a great weekend. We swam. We water-skied. We tubed. We grilled out. We cooked s'mores on the fire. Funny what you remember when time slows down. I remember I was able to get up on one ski that morning (and it was the first time I was able to slalom ski since before my daughter was born). We took family photos which turned out really great. We all looked so perfect and happy. Little did I know what was coming!

Fast forward a few hours. The extended family had all left to start their drives home. Our kids were beat from playing so hard all weekend with their cousins, and went to bed early. My ex- and I were finally alone. We get some fabulous displays of heat lightning in the Georgia summer and it's always so cool to see the lightning flash across the lake. He asked me if I wanted to sit outside on the porch with him to watch the lightning. Of course I did. I was thrilled he asked. When we first got the lake house, we used to love to sit outside together and just talk and talk! We had gotten out of that habit as of late. He asked, and I jumped at the chance.

I remember sitting together snuggled up on our porch swing, both of us swinging side by side in the dark. I remember talking about his new job and how much he was enjoying it. I remember talking about how excited I was that we were finally going to be together as a family again. I remember the night got chillier and I snuggled closer. His arm was around me as we rocked and talked. We even sat silently in what I took as the normal silence of a couple who is content to just enjoy one another in silence. I remember thinking, "I'm going to get lucky tonight." I felt a level of intimacy and closeness with him that I hadn't felt in a while. I snuggled a bit deeper and rested my head in his lap. And that's when it all started.

He asked, "How do you think we are doing?" I knew from the tone of his voice that this wasn't the kind of question designed to elicit a deep conversation about our love for one another. I instantly got goosebumps. I pushed myself up off his lap and looked in his eyes. "What do you mean, 'how do you think we are doing?'" I rhetorically questioned back. I then continued, "I think life has been really rough with you living in Denver for the past seven months, but I think life is about to be great now that we'll be there with you in five weeks." Then I asked the obvious question that he wanted me to ask, "Why? How do YOU think we are doing?"

His response was shocking in that it made absolutely no sense to me. He started rambling, saying things like, "I just don't love you. I don't think I've ever been in love with you. I've felt this way since the day we were married. I've thought about divorce on and off over the years. It's all me. I've never learned how to love. I just feel a general sense of despair. Life should have more meaning. I'm only 80% happy (that was my favorite one – do you know how many people would LOVE to feel 80% happy!?!??!). You deserve someone who loves you more. I want you to be happy. I need to figure out how to love someone else. I'm incapable of loving someone else."

I went from thinking I was going to get lucky that night, to feeling like the most unlucky woman in the world. It sucked. Nothing else to say about it. It just sucked. I think I cried, talked, yelled, and cried some more, just simply trying to understand where he was coming from until I finally fell into bed at 2 a.m. I didn't sleep much that night. He slept next to me while I tossed and turned. A few hours later, he got up and left for a flight. He had a business trip scheduled to Michigan. After he was ready to go, he stood in the doorway of our bedroom and simply said, "Goodbye, Monique" and left for a week. Our marriage was over.

That conversation, held on the rocking chair on the porch at the lake house, became known as "The Pronouncement." That was my personal D-Day. "The Pronouncement" will always resonate with me. It was the day my life, and the lives of my two precious children, changed forever.

Bottom line: Always give your best to your husband and never take anything for granted. When you are feeling your worst, that's when you get to know yourself the best. Make sure the "you" you get to know is on the high road.

Discovering The Midlife Crisis: Just Buy A Red Convertible And Be Done With It!

"All seasons are beautiful for the person who carries happiness within."

~ Horace Friess

If your husband has just told you he is leaving, you are probably feeling as though someone either punched you in the stomach, stabbed you in the back — or both. It's a crazy concoction of anger, sadness, denial, devastation, shock, grief, anxiety, fear, pain, resentment, disgust and a complete loss of self-esteem. Guess what? You are not alone.

When my ex- first said those words, "I don't love you, I've never loved you," I freaked out. Who says that? Especially after 16 years of marriage! As I've come to discover, that phrase is absolutely classic in its delivery. As I've shared my story with others, and they have shared their story with me, there is a very common theme. Almost every woman going through a divorce has heard that same phrase or something like it.

All relationships have their ups and downs, their peaks and valleys, and we consider this a normal part of the seasons of marriage. We work through them and we move forward ... together. It goes without saying that marriage is hard work, and it does take two people willing to make the investment on a daily basis.

Hindsight being 20/20, I realize that my ex- and I had definitely drifted apart. I shrugged it off. Looking at most of my friends in this stage of our lives, who hadn't grown apart from their spouses with all the craziness of raising kids, working, volunteering, etc.? I told myself that this too would pass and that this was a stage in life and definitely a stage in marriage. I had seen friends get through this "stage" when their kids were older and more self-sufficient and then I had seen marriages re-spark and rekindle. I held out hope, actually, it was more than hope, I held onto confident knowledge that the same would be true for us. I couldn't have been more wrong.

From an early age, we taught our kids to obey the golden rule: "Do unto others as you want them to do to you." A few years earlier, we had created our "Family Resolutions" on New Year's Day and many of them focused on treating one another with trust and respect. We printed the family credo on nice paper, each penned our signatures, and hung them in our rooms. They read as follows:

Family Resolutions

1. We don't always get what we want, and we will only ask once.

2. We will always greet one another in the morning with a loving greeting.

3. We will do our morning routine every day ... get dressed, make our bed, clean our room, brush our teeth, wash our face and hands.

4. We will never lie, cheat or steal.

5. In all activities, we will be good sports.

6. We will each read at least 20 minutes every day.

7. We will always use manners ... say please and thank you, use table manners, say excuse me, look people in the eye when we speak, and shake hands when introducing ourselves.

8. We will always make sure the Internet is safe.

9. We will remember that we are individuals.

10. We will always wear our helmets when on a bike, skateboard, roller-skates, scooter, etc.

11. We will do our homework without fighting, with a smile, and before we play.

12. We will always support and stand up for one another.

13. We will always be kind to others.

14. We will not whine or be sassy.

15. We will go to bed (on school nights) between 7:30 and 8:00 PM ... lights off ... no coming in and out of our rooms and procrastinating!

16. In exchange for obeying our Family Resolutions, we will get $2.25 in allowance each week; of that, we pay God $.25, the bank $1.00, and we get $1.00.

Unfortunately, so many of these basic family resolutions seem to fly out the window when divorce happens. Not sure why different rules should apply, but they do. Rules 4, 12, and 13 seem to get violated the most when a husband and wife are divorcing. I have seen it happen time and time and time again. Lies happen. Hateful words are exchanged. We're only human. Of course we react emotionally when our emotions are attacked.

At the end of the day, however, how can we expect our children to follow the rules if we aren't modeling that same behavior? It's an interesting dichotomy. Taking the high road, being a role model, are themes you will see peppered throughout this book. There isn't, nor should there be, one set of rules for adults, and another set for kids, when it comes to basic treatment of others, right?

When I heard those words, "I'm just not happy … I've never loved you …" I was shocked. Turns out, those words are classic signs of a midlife crisis. Studies on the male midlife crisis show that most men exhibit certain signs, and it's kind of creepy how similarly it all unfolds.

I know several people who have married and divorced within just a few years because they quickly realized they had made a mistake in marrying and they truly weren't meant to be together. In every case, these couples have come to the same decision together, maturely sat down and discussed their options, and have ended their marriages amicably. Most of these situations happened to people who were married for less than five years, and thankfully most of them involved marriages with no children. This chapter isn't about those marriages.

While society tends to joke about the "midlife crisis" and depicts the middle-aged, balding man, driving a red convertible, research does actually support this notion of a crisis that many men experience in "middle-age." If you talk to middle-aged women who have experienced divorce, you will find that many of them will tell you their spouse changed overnight and became someone who discarded all that was once important to him for a new life that was all about what he wanted.

So often, women internalize these changes and start to think there is something "wrong" with them. If only I was skinnier, or prettier, or a better cook, or worked more, or dressed differently, or played golf, or … and we try and change who we are (and who our husbands first fell in love with) in an attempt to make them more content. Perhaps it's time we stopped trying to change who we are and start trying to determine the real cause of the discontent.

We joke about the midlife crisis (when it's really not a laughing matter – just look at how many people are getting divorced), but what exactly is it?

A midlife crisis is most often experienced between the ages of 40 and 60. It was first identified by the psychologist Carl Jung and is a normal part of the maturing process. Of course, most people will experience some form of emotional transition during that time of life, but it's how they deal with it that makes it a crisis situation or just another emotional transition to overcome.

For some, a midlife crisis is more complicated. It can be a really uncomfortable time where everything seems to be turned upside down. Many times, people suffer depression and need to see a therapist or counselor. Often times the crisis makes people act in ways that are seemingly outrageous to their normal expected behavior, and that clearly, often leads to divorce. According to the About.com guide to divorce support, people going through a midlife crisis often experience a range of feelings such as:

Emotions Surrounding a Midlife Crisis

~ Unhappiness with life and the lifestyle that may have provided them with happiness for many years.

~ Boredom with people and things that may have been of interest to them before.

~ Feeling a need for adventure and change.

~ Questioning the choices, they have made in their lives and the validity of decisions they made years before.

~ Confusion about who they are and where they are going.

~ Anger at their spouse and blame for feeling tied down.

~ Unable to make decisions about where they want to go with their life.

~ Doubt that they ever loved their spouse and resentment over the marriage.

~ A desire for a new and passionate, intimate relationships.

Not everyone who has a difficult time adjusting to midlife needs to transition into crisis mode. Experts think those that cross the line into "crisis" do so because of other external factors that push them over the edge. These factors may be other stressors that exacerbate the midlife crisis or some sort of childhood issues that resurface because they were never dealt with properly in the past.

In *How to SURVIVE Your Husband's Midlife Crisis*, authors Gay Courter and Pat Gaudette provide a "Midlife Crisis Quiz." Naturally, the more points you score, the more likely it is that some sort of midlife crisis may be looming on the horizon.

How many vulnerability factors is your man exhibiting?

(Check the heart next to each statement you agree with)

♡ He is on either side of his fortieth (or fiftieth) birthday.

♡ He is showing concerns about getting "old."

♡ He had bought a more youthful wardrobe.

♡ He is coloring his hair or trying a trendier cut.

♡ He has started working out.

♡ He reminisces about his teen years or "when he was younger."

♡ He listens to romantic songs from his dating years.

♡ He talks about his "first love" and wonders "what if?"

♡ He yearns for a sportier vehicle (or has bought one).

♡ He doesn't find enjoyment in the usual leisure-time activities.

♡ He wants to do something adventurous like hand-gliding or auto racing.

♡ He is bored with life.

♡ He questions the meaning of his life.

♡ He is dissatisfied with his job or career.

♡ He feels trapped by responsibilities or obligations to others.

♡ He has financial problems.

♡ He worries about the future.

♡ He suddenly wants another child.

♡ He is unhappy that the children are grown and on their own.

♡ He has some major health problems.

♡ He has experienced the death of a parent, close friend or other family member.

♡ He is frequently nervous and/or irritable.

♡ He criticizes his wife and marriage.

♡ He is not interested in sex.

♡ He is occasionally impotent.

♡ He feels inadequate.

♡ He say he loves his wife but isn't "in love" with her.

♡ He is uncharacteristically abusive.

♡ He worries about everything to excess.

♡ His sleeping habits have changed.

♡ He drinks more or is experimenting with drugs.

♡ He feels that life no longer has any purpose.

♡ He is concerned about death and dying.

♡ He talks about suicide in the near or far future.

Total Score_____

SCORING:

~ Less than 5 may indicate normal aging issues.

~ 6-10 indicate more worrisome issues.

~ 11-15 suggest he has some serious midlife issues.

~ 16 or more indicate a crisis is on the immediate horizon.

A word of caution: don't read this list, count up the items, and totally freak out. Every man is going to (hopefully) have the first item on the list at some point (that is, being on either side of turning 40 or 50 years old). Most people, men and women, express some sort of feeling about getting older. There is a distinction between things on this last that simply "happen to us" and those more "proactive" things that we do. Use your own interpretation as you review this list and recognize that these are thought-provokers, not absolutes.

I've talked with different women, and we've compared notes about the "common" things our husbands told us as we realized it was the beginning of the end. More than once I've said, "I feel like you overheard our conversation." The consistency of messages was frightening, and the standard phrases were comical. The conversations sound something like this, "We're drifting apart. I don't know what I want. It isn't you. It's not about you; it's about me. I haven't been happy for a long time. I don't know what love is. I'm not fulfilled. I don't miss you at all. You deserve someone better than me."

We all have guardrails in our lives — those barriers, or edges, which exist that keep us on the straight and narrow, on the "right" path. Divorce is often ugly, nasty, and mean. Nobody wants to feel rejected and unloved. So frequently I hear, "I just don't love my wife anymore. We've grown apart." I encourage people to have this conversation with their spouse before they make the next bad decision which is often acting on that lack of intimacy, that lack of connection, and that lack of love, with someone else. When that happens, what can be a valid concern between two married people, the need to reconnect, leads to what can be a disastrous result with ramifications that will last forever.

Those of you who are feeling "out of love" with your spouse and considering divorce, please do two things. One, talk with your husband about it and let him know exactly where you stand so that no one gets blind sided. Two, take the high road. I wish my ex-husband had come to me and said, "I'm not feeling it anymore. Something's wrong. I'm not in love with you and we need to figure this out together." It may have still led to divorce, who knows. Instead, I got blind sided with a decision that I knew ultimately was already made. He had no intentions of working on our marriage. He clearly had decided he was done. He simply hadn't let me in on that decision yet. Poor choices were made, and the consequences of those choices will exist forever.

I've had girlfriends come to me using that same line that is classically heard from men. They say, "I don't love my husband. I don't know if I ever have. I'm not happy. I'm not fulfilled ..." I warn each and every one of them to go communicate with their husbands before they cross that proverbial guardrail and do something they will regret for the rest of their lives in the form of lying or cheating.

I've often asked this rhetorical question to people who come to me with this concept of "I just don't love my husband (or wife) anymore ..." If your son or daughter acts the way you are acting right now when they grow up, would you be proud of them? If your son or daughter is treated by someone else the way you are treating another person right now, would you be pleased for them? Putting ourselves in someone else's shoes, particularly those of our children who will one day become adults, often serves to make our decisions a bit clearer.

I look at is this way. If this person was important enough to you at some point in your life to merit you marrying them, then it's safe to assume there was some level of love (or like) which existed. What could possibly change that basic fundamental human value of respecting that person (often the mother or father of your children) that would merit you not communicating openly with that person and instead would rationalize you lying to them?

We taught our kids that no matter what happens to them in their lives, if they respond the "right" way, they will never have reason to be ashamed, embarrassed, or imprisoned! We taught them that their reputations were key, and managing those reputations was an important job. Both my kids have a sign hanging in their rooms that says, "Integrity is doing the right thing even when no one else is looking." Taking the high road is expected. It is non-negotiable now or in the future.

Bottom line: Respect, trust and open communication are guardrails in our lives, foundational to a strong marriage, and a basic tenet of taking the high road.

Giving Your Best To Your Spouse:
Show Love And Respect Every Single Day!

"The more you invest
in a marriage,
the more valuable
it becomes."

~ Amy Grant

Respect, trust and open communication truly are foundational to all great marriages. Marriage is hard work ... constantly. All marriages go through their peaks and valleys, their trials and tribulations, and as mine was clearly hitting a deep valley, it forced me to become introspective and really examine my role. As I looked around, I saw a general lack of respect in many marriages on the part of one or both spouses to expend that extra amount of energy to make the other person feel respected and loved.

Was I cheating on my husband? Absolutely not – in the way that most of you are defining it. But as I thought about it, and looked around, it occurred to me that "cheating" can occur in other ways.

Have you cheated on your husband by spending all of your time and devoting all of your energy to your children? Have you cheated on your husband by becoming obsessed with work? Have you cheated on your husband by getting emotionally attached to Facebook® and spending hours glued to the screen each day? Volunteering? Going to the gym? Talking on the phone to your girlfriends? Are you so busy doing "other" things, all of which are very important (OK – perhaps not Facebook®, but certainly caring for your kids) that you put to the side burner the very person who should take a prominent role in your life? We often avoid addressing issues or problems in our marriages and simply opt to not deal with them by becoming so involved in everything else going on around us.

Neither side can afford to get lazy in a marriage, and I often think we do get lazy because we get caught up in all of the other responsibilities of life that we assume our spouse will be the most forgiving and tolerant.

When I was a student in law school, I recall a professor distributing an article (still not sure why!) that was essentially teed up as being a reprint from a periodical called *Housekeeping Monthly*, dated May 13, 1955. It claimed that the list was from a 1950's home economics textbook intended for high school girls to teach them how to prepare for married life. You may have seen this. It has certainly made its way across the Internet and I see it resurface every few years. It often comes attached to a photo purported to be from the 1950's of a man in a three-piece suit ostensibly walking in the door from work to find his 1950's wife standing before the stove cooking dinner while looking perfectly coiffed in her dress and pumps. Their two young children are playing at her side. It's all smiles and, well, it's all perfect.

For the most part, we all know this isn't the reality of life today. As wives and mothers, we may be more familiar with the late afternoon/early evening chaos of making sure the kids are doing their homework, getting them ready for their after-school activities or sports, and simultaneously trying to figure what to throw together for dinner. When the husband/father walks in the door, it may be a scene of chaos.

If you haven't seen the article before, here is the list intended to help girls prepare for married life:

A 1950's Housewife

~ Have dinner ready. Plan ahead, even the night before, to have a delicious meal ready, on time for his return. This is a way of letting him know that you have been thinking about him and are concerned about his needs. Most men are hungry when they come home and the prospect of a good meal (especially his favorite dish) is part of the warm welcome needed.

~ Prepare yourself. Take 15 minutes to rest so that you'll be refreshed when he arrives. Touch up your make-up, put a ribbon in your hair and be fresh-looking. He has just been with a lot of work-weary people.

~ Be a little gay and a little more interesting for him. His boring day may need a lift and one of your duties is to provide it.

~ Clear away the clutter. Make one last trip through the main part of the house just before your husband arrives.

~ Gather up schoolbooks, toys, papers, etc. and then run a dustcloth over the tables.

~ Over the cooler months of the year you should prepare and light a fire for him to unwind by. Your husband will feel he has reached a haven of rest and order, and it will give you a lift too. After all, catering for his comfort will provide you with immense personal satisfaction.

~ Prepare the children. Take a few minutes to wash the children's hands and faces (if they are small), comb their hair and, if necessary, change their clothes. They are little treasures and he would like to see them playing the part. Minimize all noise.

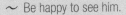

~ Be happy to see him.

~ Greet him with a warm smile and show sincerity in your desire to please him.

~ Listen to him. You may have a dozen important things to tell him, but the moment of his arrival is not the time. Let him talk first – remember, his topics of conversation are more important than yours.

~ Make the evening his. Never complain if he comes home late or goes out to dinner, or other places of entertainment without you. Instead, try to understand his world of strain and pressure and his very real need to be at home and relax.

~ Your goal: Try to make sure your home is a place of peace, order and tranquility where your husband can renew himself in body and spirit.

~ Don't greet him with complaints and problems.

~ Don't complain if he's late home for dinner or even if he stays out all night *(note from Monique, this comment strikes me as most absurd!)*. Count this as minor compared to what he might have gone through that day.

~ Make him comfortable. Have him lean back in a comfortable chair or have him lie down in the bedroom. Have a cool or warm drink ready for him.

~ Arrange his pillow and offer to take off his shoes. Speak in a low, soothing and pleasant voice.

~ Don't ask him questions about his actions or question his judgment or integrity. Remember, he is the master of the house and as such will always exercise his will with fairness and truthfulness. You have no right to question him.

~ A good wife always knows her place.

When I first read this article I was mortified by it and laughed. I was a career woman. I saw the article as old-fashioned and degrading to the treatment of women as equals. I was thankful to be a woman in the '90's and not the '50's. Naturally I began to look at it through the eyes of my mom who became a wife and mother in the 1960's. I considered my mom to be a traditional wife and mother and she and my dad were married over 30 years before my dad passed away. I began to look at the little things that she did for my dad day in and day out. I began to see things that my dad did for my mom day in and day out. I began to see elements of the article, that if taken in the appropriate context, did make absolute sense. Hold on! Don't get all bent out of shape – hear me out!

You know what I think? There is something very real and valid to this article that should be applied to both husbands and wives. Imagine if every wife and every husband adopted even half of these "suggested practices" in how they dealt with their spouse each and every day. The level of love and respect and communication that would be demonstrated would be phenomenal. The intentional behavior changes this would drive would ultimately save many marriages.

This isn't about the role of stay-at-home moms versus working moms. This isn't about who brings home a larger share of the family income. This isn't about women being subservient. This is simply about respect.

What if every time you walked in the door, your husband got up from whatever he was doing and came over to give you a kiss and a hug?

What if every time you had something you wanted to share with your husband, he listened to you and made you feel like what you were saying was the most important thing happening at that moment?

What if your husband made sure he looked good when he knew you were about to come home – nothing major, just brushed his hair, perhaps put on some deodorant, or a splash of that cologne that used to drive you crazy when you were dating?

What if your husband made an effort to clear away the clutter that comes from running a busy household – the school bags, the sports gear, the stack of mail and newspapers?

What if every so often your husband fluffed the pillow on the couch for you, took off your shoes, gave you a little foot massage, and brought you a cold drink? Who knows what might happen!

I would bet that you would feel loved and respected. And I'm willing to bet the same is true for your husband if you did these things as well. When you think about it, there are many elements of the article that promote the basics of love and respect in a marriage. Think about when you were dating. Doing the little things didn't seem like such a big deal, did it? Most women I have spoken with said that when they were first married, they went out of their way to do special things for their husbands. Naturally! And, most of the time their husbands chose to go out of their way to do special things for their wives.

Somewhere along the path of life, I believe many couples lose the priority of doing special things for each other. Marriage doesn't become intentional. I look at couples who I believe still have a really, solid marriage and I see a constant desire on the part of both the husband and the wife to purposefully treat the other with respect.

By the way, the general consensus on this list is that it wasn't originally printed in a home economics textbook. Said textbook has never been found! Whatever the true source may be, it's certainly become a document with incredible staying power thanks to the Internet. Take it with a grain of salt ... but do consider some of the points which you deem valid.

Your Personal 1950's Checklist

What are 5 little things I used to do for my husband (ex-)
that I stopped doing in recent years?

1.

2.

3.

4.

5.

Why did I stop?

What are 5 little things I would truly appreciate my husband doing for me on a regular basis?

1.

2.

3.

4.

5.

Why? What would it mean to me?

Bottom line: Don't get caught up in the extremes of the article. Instead, take a moment to focus on how you would feel if your husband treated you like that every day. Take a moment to focus on how your husband would feel if you treated him like that every day. There's something to be said for that intentional love and respect that drives commitment and a healthy marriage.

Taking the High Road: It is ALL About the Best Interests of Your Children

"When you're feeling your worst, that's when you get to know yourself the best."

~ Anonymous

We hear about the "high road," but what does it really mean to take the high road? It's like the signs in my kids' rooms: it means, "doing the right thing even when no one else is looking." It means treating others the way you would want to be treated, even when they have hurt you badly. It means that your behavior passes the "newspaper" test and that you never did anything you wouldn't want to see in print on the front page. It means being able to look in the mirror each and every day for the rest of your life with the assurance that you didn't cross over your personal guardrails and that you stayed true to the person you want to be.

Sophia Loren said, "When you are a mother, you are never really alone in your thoughts. A mother always has to think twice, once for herself and once for her child" Bingo! That's exactly it. Every decision I made came down to what I thought about it, and what my children would think about it. As I speak with women about their experiences going through divorce, one thing becomes glaringly obvious. If we use the filter of "what's best for my children," it becomes pretty clear what decisions need to be made, or what actions need to be carried out. That's not to say it becomes easy, just that it becomes clear! Every decision you make, every statement you utter, every action you take, if made, spoken or taken with the best interests of your children (their best honest intentions!), will serve to guide you, almost your own moral compass, for how to behave.

It's validating to speak with so many women and see where they are in their journey of divorce. I love to be able to see where they are, show them where I am, and help them to understand that they will survive, and thrive, despite what seem to be overwhelming hurdles at the current moment.

The obvious intentions of this are clear and simple. Things like "never bad-mouth" your ex- in front of the kids or never tell the kids "what daddy did." But, this guiding principle applies in so many other ways as well.

How many of you have fantasized about your soon-to-be-ex- being killed in a freak car accident, or perhaps fantasized about killing him yourself? You aren't a normal woman going through a tumultuous divorce if these thoughts haven't entered your mind at some point. Laugh! It's normal, and every woman I know has thought it at some point.

One of my friends who was going through her own divorce called me one Saturday night at about 11:45PM. "Monique," she cried out, "I'm a terrible person! I keep thinking how much better off I would be if Mark (name changed, of course) was dead! How can I think things like this? He's the father of my kids. I'm a horrible person!" She was truly distraught. Ask any therapist or divorce care counselor - this is a normal thought. Think about how much easier it would be if you didn't have to deal with him anymore. A word of caution ... never act on this desire, no matter how tempting!

I'm a firm believer in doing everything humanly possible to make your marriage work. I don't believe in divorce as an easy way out. I'm not a proponent of divorce. It's hurtful and hateful. As I said earlier, I knew I had to do every single thing I possibly could to save my marriage so that I could honestly tell my kids in the future that I had tried. I also knew that once I knew for sure that my marriage was over, that I would get through the divorce as quickly and painlessly as possible for all involved, with grace, dignity and integrity guiding my actions. I would take the high road.

After "The Pronouncement" as I was struggling to make sense of everything, I suggested to my ex- that we go to marriage counseling. He wasn't exactly supportive of the idea, but he agreed to go. I went to a session by myself. He went to a session by himself. We went to a session together.

We sat with our counselor for 90 minutes and participated in exercises designed to share our feelings and get our emotions on the table about what was going on. It was hard work, but I gave it my all. I tried all the different communication tips that were suggested. I tried not to cry too hard, but rather worked to keep the conversation moving forward. I told my ex- that I would stand by his side while he "figured things out" but that I needed some indication from him that he was willing to work on our marriage. Our counselor said that I couldn't make unreasonable demands, but that asking him for some sort of sign that he was willing to work on our marriage was not unreasonable. It never happened. No "signs" were given.

In fact, as we left our counselor's office and walked towards our car, my ex- started laughing, and said, "That was such a joke. Didn't you think that was funny?" I was incredulous. "No," I responded, "I see nothing funny at all about what we just sat through. Our marriage is in trouble and you are laughing?" He told me not to take myself so seriously. He thought the communication process we had just been "taught" and had practiced was ridiculous. I was beginning to see that perhaps this was absolutely hopeless.

At some point I felt I was left with no choices. In a sense, I suppose, I declared my ultimatum. I said, "If you can give me a .00000000000001%

chance that you are willing to make our marriage work, then I am all in. We will move to Denver, we will work on our marriage and I will do all in my power to help you to feel fulfilled and to figure out what love is. I will give you space. I will be patient (and you know I'm not a patient person). But, if you can't give me that .0000000000001% chance that you are even willing to try, then I am not going to move across the country with our children to Denver." Funny ... he couldn't answer that question ... which I guess was an answer in and of itself. Decision made.

When I suggest to women that taking the high road means keeping knowledge that you have about your husband to yourself, their immediate reaction is that's it unfair. Why shouldn't his parents know what he's done? Why shouldn't our friends know what he's done? Why should he be able to laugh and carry-on with showing any guilt or remorse? Thoughts like this eat people up from the inside-out.

At the end of the day, when you share what you know with the world at large, or yell and scream, or attack with golf clubs, or react in any other negative way, your kids may eventually see it and that's not the behavior you want to role model for them. More importantly, your behavior will only serve to antagonize already tumultuous relations with their father which will inadvertently affect them. Being really hateful and spiteful before the divorce is finalized isn't good for the kids to see, and will only make the negotiations of divorce even more emotional and nasty than they naturally are. And, by acting out, your husband will feel completely justified in validating his own behavior, "See, you are such a b****, this is why you drove me to leave you; if you weren't such a mean person, I never would have done this ..." Don't provide any fodder for the tables to be turned against you.

By taking the high road in dealing with your attorney, his attorney, the mediator, the judge, the child advocates and whomever else may be involved in your divorce, you will build relationships as the stable woman who is truly looking out for the best interests of her kids. People don't want to "take sides," but we naturally do. We "side" with the person whom we like or who is clearly handling the difficult situation gracefully.

Women ask me if they can share their grief and hatred once the divorce is final when the negotiations are over. It's almost like victim's rights, and they want an opportunity to say their piece and be heard. The answer, of course, is yes! Legally, you can say whatever you would like and since the paperwork has been signed, there aren't any concerns about the potential ramifications. However, I would argue that it still behooves you to show some restraint. While the divorce may be over, there is still the ongoing issue of co-parenting, and again, the more tense the relationship is between the two parents, the more the children will feel that angst and have to suffer the consequences of it.

When cheating is involved, women tell me about their desire to confront the "other woman," and call her all sorts of nasty names. Again, I ask, "What good would that serve?" Let's say this woman becomes a regular fixture in the lives of your children. Do you want her to hate you so much because of what you said to her that she takes it out on your children? I would much rather have a step-mother whom my children love, than have someone whom they hate. Every child is haunted by the story of Cinderella and the wicked step-mother who cared for her own daughters so much, while making Cinderella clean the toilets! At this point, women say to me, "I will NEVER be able to do this." And I say, "YES you will!" Keep reading! It's amazing what strength we can pull when our "mom" gene kicks into gear and we know that we have to do what's right by our kids. We are women, hear us roar!

And, we are human!

As much as I promised that I would never act negatively towards my ex- in front of my kids, I also recognize that I'm human, and there were times where I wasn't able to successfully keep a handle on my emotions.

My advice is that it is perfectly OK to share emotions with your kids. I wanted my kids to know that I was sad about having problems with my marriage, but it's a balancing act with showing emotions positively and throwing your ex- under the bus.

There were just a couple of times during the course of all this mess that I did not practice what I had promised about my behavior in front of the kids. One time was during that purgatory of time where you are having serious problems, but you are still living together. We had planned to take the kids to the fireworks show one night, and given my ex's behavior earlier that evening, I decided I wasn't going to go. I told the kids to put their toys away and get their shoes on. I went out on the back porch and my ex- came out to see if I was ready. I told him I wasn't going.

He asked me why I wasn't going to the fireworks and I just started yelling at him telling him that he was ruining our family, ruining our lives, that he was selfish, that he was mean, that he could go f*** himself. The kids heard me yelling. They saw me crying. I saw them come around the corner and I stopped doing both. I tried to put a smile on my face, I gave them a hug, and I told them to have a good time at the fireworks. And, I felt horrible for them.

I'm not proud of what I said that night. I still wish it hadn't happened. To this day, I hate that it happened and that they heard what I said. It wasn't fair of me to put them in that position.

If you are human, you will most likely cross the line and say something at some point that you wish you could take back – especially in front of your kids. My advice? Don't try to deny it. Don't try to justify it. Deal with it. Apologize to your kids. And, try not to let it happen again!

At the end of the day, do all you can to work on your marriage and keep it healthy. If it's already a marriage in trouble, then do all you can to repair and restore it. However, when the time comes that you absolutely know in your heart that it isn't going to work, then move forward with integrity.

As marriages fail, I've seen too many people get stuck between what they know in their head is the right decision, and what they feel in their heart. Do all you can, but know when to move on. My mantra became, "I can't control what happens to me; I can only control how I react to it." I lived by this principle. I had absolutely no control over what was happening to my marriage, and as a woman who likes to be in control, this was frightening, but, as I said to my kids, I could control how I reacted to it, and I vowed to react and respond as best as I could.

Bottom line: Do all you can to make absolutely certain that your marriage is over before you give up on it … you owe this to yourself and your children! Always take the high road!

GETTING THE WORD OUT:
WHY IS TELLING MOM SO TOUGH?

"A mother is one to
whom you hurry
when you are troubled."

~ Emily Dickinson

"God could not be everywhere,
so he created mothers."

~ Jewish Proverb

The days and weeks and months following "The Pronouncement" were an absolute blur. I tried to absorb it all and tried to understand it. It made no sense. My calibration became doing whatever it took to make decisions that were in the best interest of my kids. This is a consistent message I hear from all the mothers with whom I speak: "I want to take care of my kids! I don't want them to be harmed by this." As mothers, we care for our children, and that doesn't change if our kids are in preschool, elementary school, or all grown up. My mom's first reaction was to take care of me.

Initially, I only told two of my dearest friends, Kathleen and Ann, what my ex- had said to me. Kathleen and I have been friends since we were ten years old and she's the closest thing I have to a sister. She had known my ex- from the day we started dating. Ann and I had been friends for 12 years and talked regularly. Their husbands were friends with my ex-. The six of us and our families did a lot together. I trusted them implicitly and I knew they would keep everything I said confidential. I valued their opinions. I needed their support.

Telling your best friends shouldn't be difficult, but it is. It's as if verbalizing it makes it that much more real. If you ignore it, perhaps it will go away. I've known women whose husbands have told them, "I don't love you and I want a divorce," and they have kept it to themselves for weeks and weeks, hoping they will wake up from the nightmare that sits before them. The reality is that the nightmare seldom disappears. Regardless of who initiated it, you still feel like a failure, like you couldn't keep your marriage together.

My advice is to be selective on who you tell as you start to share what is happening to you, particularly during the first couple of weeks as you may still be reeling from the shock and trying to figure out what is going on. Divorce should be a relatively private affair for the good of the children involved, and frankly for the good of all the relationships it impacts.

As a practical matter, think of the implications of telling a whole group of people about your marital problems, and the impact it will have on you if you and your husband do decide to reconcile. Things will have been said that are painful and hurtful, and frankly, that are impossible to retract. It's better to have just a few key people as your sounding board during the initial stages of shock and anger, and these key people should be those best girlfriends that you have and the ones you trust the most to be there for you, to listen, to provide advice, and to comfort you.

Yet another reason to not share your marital issues with too many people is that divorce is a juicy topic that fuels gossip. I hated feeling like the status of my relationship with my husband was the topic of conversation all over town. I hated knowing people were talking about me. I worried about what my kids would hear, not from me, but from their friends and their friends' parents.

Telling Kathleen and Ann was difficult, but by far the most difficult call I had to make was to my mom. She had just left us at the lake house and we'd had a great weekend. We had said our good-byes pending our move to Denver, and yet here I was calling her to tell her what had happened. I knew she was going to be so incredibly disappointed. She loved my ex- like a son. How would she react to this? I knew she was going to be sad, angry, disappointed, shocked, and scared all at the same time.

Many mothers and daughters share a special bond. I have heard from several friends who have also been divorced that telling their moms was one of the hardest parts. I'm not sure why. Perhaps at our core, we are all still those little girls worried about "disappointing" our parents.

I have a friend who was never particularly close to her mom. They battled more than the norm during those awkward teenage years when we try to assert our independence, and really never built back a closeness and a trust. Yet calling to tell her mom that she and her husband were getting divorced was one of the hardest calls she ever made. She waited a few months after her husband had moved out before she made the call, and even then, she said she just started crying and crying on the phone.

I love my mom dearly. We talk several times a week. We are very close and I would never do anything to create stress for her. Yet, I knew this would cause great worry and distress. As a parent, I totally understand that feeling of wanting to protect your children from all harm. I knew mom would want to protect me, when in reality there was nothing she could do. Honestly, I didn't want to call her. It's like the teenager who finds out she is pregnant but hopes that by ignoring the situation, as opposed to facing reality, it might go away. I wanted this to go away, and I knew it wouldn't.

I waited a few days to call her and I practiced what I would say over and over. You know how when your child falls and hurts himself and you aren't right there, he acts OK and doesn't really cry? But, as soon as he sees you, he just loses it and cries (even if the hurt is gone by then)? I learned that as a 39 year-old adult the reflex is the same. I got myself together that night and called my mom. And, as soon as she answered the phone and said hello, I started bawling and hyperventilating. She didn't know what was going on. She didn't know if I was hurt, or if something had happened to the kids or to my husband.

I managed to sputter out in short staccato bursts of air "I'm ...O ... K ... no ... body ... is ... hurt ... hold on ... I ... need ... to ... catch ... my ... breath ..." It was awful. My poor mom. She had to listen to me hyperventilating, not knowing what was going on, but clearly with a sinking feeling that she was about to hear something tragic. My mom knows I don't cry a whole lot, and I certainly don't cry to the extent that I hyperventilate. The last time I had done that was when my dad had died eight years earlier. It took me several minutes to gain my composure. It felt like hours.

My mom was the wonderful, amazing person whom I've always known her to be. She was supportive of me. She was just as confused about the entire situation as I was, especially having just left us all a few days earlier. She kicked into problem-solving mode and asked all the right questions about whether we were seeing a counselor, about whether we were still moving, about what we were going to do about our living situation. But most of all, she listened and provided a reassuring message that everything would be OK and that she would be there for the kids and me no matter what happened. I know she didn't sleep for days. She's a mom, and she was worried about her little girl. Telling my mom was hard, but having her support and love was amazing.

As a mom, you would do whatever you need to do to keep your kids safe from harm, right? The same is true at any age. Once a mom, always a mom!

As the weeks progressed, I turned to my best friends, my mom, and my minister. My ex- and I put a plan together to tell our children (that's the next chapter!). Now, I knew we had to tell our extended circle of friends. We had to let people know what was going on and that we weren't moving to Denver. My friends were on the ball. The planning for our going-away party was well-underway and the invitations had already been ordered.

I crafted an email that we sent to our larger circle of friends from the neighborhood, church, and other social networks. I wrote that we were having some issues, and that we had delayed our decision to move. We asked that they please respect our privacy for the well-being of our children, and to please keep us in their prayers. I can only imagine how many people we absolutely shocked when they opened and read that email.

When word got out that we were having issues, people were surprised. If I had a nickel for every person who said "we never thought this would happen to you," I would have been able to pay for my divorce attorney entirely! They reacted and wanted to talk about it. The worst part was knowing that I was the subject of lots of behind the scenes conversations. People love scoop, they love gossip, they love drama, and divorce covers the gamut. People speculated about what was happening, about who had initiated it, whether there was some "event" that started the ball rolling. Take the high road. I asked Kathleen and Ann to help manage the drama and keep this off the rumor circuit.

Bottom line: Our moms want to protect us from hurt ... whether the "boo-boo's" come from falling off your bike and scraping your knee or come from having your heart broken. Craft your communication plan wisely – rely on a few trusted friends, and have them help you manage the drama.

Telling the Kids:
The Most Difficult Thing You
Will Ever Have To Do

*"What we are teaches the child
far more than what we say,
so we must be what we want
our children to become."*

~ Anonymous

Once a mom, always a mom, and no mom ever wants to intentionally hurt her children either physically, emotionally or spiritually. I awoke the morning in which we were going to tell our kids what was going on with such a headache and such a feeling of dread. I absolutely hated the conversation that I knew we had to have with them. We had to tell them that we weren't moving. My ex- wanted to give them a message that, "Mom and Dad are having some problems and that you guys are going to stay with Mom in Atlanta until we figure it out." He wanted to tell the kids that we were "separated." I was adamant that I was not going to participate in that message since I knew it was a bunch of false hope and BS.

After the "joke" of a session with the counselor, I knew in my gut that he had no interest and no intention whatsoever of working on our marriage. I knew that there would be no "trial separation." I wanted hope, and never got it. I wasn't going to give my kids any measure of false hope and create more pain.

Remember the prologue? At the end of the day, it is all about making sure the kids feel safe, secure and loved by both parents. I also knew that all the books on divorce talk about how important it is to deliver the message to your kids together. He had done some reading as well and academically we both knew how this conversation was "supposed" to flow. We knew that we had to talk with the kids together. He knew my perspective and where I was coming from. I said, "Don't tell the kids we are separated if you know it is ultimately going to end in divorce. Don't you dare give them false hope."

I wasn't sure what he was going to say when we called the kids together that Saturday morning, I just know that it was one of the worst days of my life and I will never, ever forget the look on the kids' faces when he started talking and they realized what was going on.

We had a tradition in our family that we called a "family meeting" whenever we needed to talk about an important issue or something that was on our minds. Only eight months earlier, we had called a family meeting to tell the kids we were moving to Denver. That Saturday morning, we called a family meeting and both kids came into the family room. My son, always the kid with the quick wit, joked, "What? Are we not moving to Denver?" He expected his joke to be laughed at. He received an entirely different reaction. Without missing a beat, my ex- said, "No. We aren't moving to Denver. Your mom and I are separated and are probably going to get a divorce." Period! Blunt! Done!

To this day, I can remember the next seconds in the most infinite detail. I can recall the look on both kids faces as they absorbed and interpreted his words. I see the detail on their faces as they both took on this look of pain and began to cry. It was absolutely horrible to watch. Writing this, it still feels absolutely horrible. It was a slow-motion nightmare. I hated him for what he was doing to our family. I hated the fact that I couldn't make this better. I hated the fact that for the rest of my life, I wouldn't be able to be with my children whenever I wanted to be with them. That I was going to have to celebrate Christmas without them. That I would not always be with them on their birthdays, or my birthday. That there would be stretches of time where I wouldn't be tucking them in and saying prayers with them at night. It was truly the most horrible of days.

The kids cried. We cried. We hugged them. We told them that while our family would be different, we would still be a family. We told them that we both loved them and that this had absolutely nothing to do with them. We told them all the "right" things that the experts advise. It didn't make it any easier. In fact, I felt like a big, fat liar! I didn't believe things were going to be all right. The kids were sad. They were angry. They didn't understand it. But, they didn't ask too many questions.

Without a doubt, that was the worst day of my life. We hurt our children. Like I said, I will NEVER forget the look on their faces as his message registered in their brains. It was awful.

I'm not an expert on "telling the kids," but I do have my opinion. I do think it is imperative that both parents are there for the conversation. I think it's vitally important that the kids don't blame themselves for the divorce. They have to know that both parents love them and that this divorce has nothing to do with them.

For me, it was the weeks and months after the "family meeting" where I, as a parent, was able to influence my kids and provide a solid, safe environment. I came to the realization pretty early that we had never really shared our emotions very openly as a family, and that this wasn't something to be proud of. My kids hadn't seen me cry too often and they certainly hadn't seen my ex- and I have "tough" discussions.

My son's first words as my ex- walked out the door the day after the family meeting were, "Mom, I don't get it. You and Dad never fight." And, he was right. We never, if rarely, raised our voices or disagreed with one another. I realized I had always held my emotions in check.

I realized our daughter was closed with her emotions and it worried me that she was keeping everything bottled up inside. I consciously decided I wasn't going to hold my emotions inside and hide them anymore — from anyone — not my kids, not my friends, not any future relationships. If something was on my mind, I was going to share it.

The months following "The Pronouncement" were horrible on my emotions. Obviously, I cried ... a lot, and I didn't try to hide this from the kids. I thought it was good for them to know that I was sad too. Can you imagine if I had hidden all my tears and they were led to assume that I considered life to be just wonderful? All things in moderation. I also wasn't crying all day every day. I made sure we had lots of discussion about the role of faith, the importance of talking to God to help us navigate through tough times, and the intense value of sharing our emotions.

The kids and I had some amazing discussions ... absolutely amazing. They opened up, we all opened up, in ways we never had before. I recall saying to some of my girlfriends that from a timing perspective, this may have been great timing with my daughter and me because it opened up some doors of communication that may have otherwise remained closed at such a pivotal pre-teen time in her life. To this day, our relationship is closer than perhaps it might have been and I am so thankful for that.

I wanted the kids to know that it was OK to cry, that it was OK to be angry, that it was OK to laugh ... and we did all of those things. I want to emphasize that I never tried to burden them with my emotions either. As the emotions came, they were witnessed, but I never made a big deal of them in terms of suppressing them and keeping them totally at bay, or in highlighting them. The waves of emotion would pass, and they were what they were.

My son, who was eight years old at the time, has always been pretty in-tune with his emotions and I used to catch him looking me deep in the eyes to see if I was tearing up. He has a very empathetic side and he would bring me a tissue or hold my hand if he saw I was crying. I remember one night in particular when he said, "Mom, you know, I have super powers!" "You do," I exclaimed, "What power is that?" And he sweetly said, "I can tell when you are sad and when I kiss you and hug you, it makes you feel better." How right he was! He did have super powers indeed. Both of my kids were the source of my power and inspiration to get through this situation — to help them get through this situation — as emotionally healthy as possible.

It's not about creating guilt for your kids, or drawing them into your own emotional nightmare. I've seen other women do that and their kids become the emotional crutches. That's not fair for children to endure. We are the parents. However, I am so pleased that my kids witnessed my emotions, shared their emotions, and learned how to face and deal with their emotions. I'd like to think this has increased all of our emotional intelligence beyond where it would have been.

I can't emphasize enough ... talk it out, communicate and over-communicate with your kids. If you have a faith, share your prayers to God out loud with your kids so they can hear what it is you are praying for. They listen to this stuff, they learn, and they role-model it. The kids and I had always prayed together at meals and before bedtime, but these prayers had historically been the rote, memorized ones and really didn't have much thought go into them. My prayers became much more specific petitions to God, much more specific thanksgivings for the little things that had gone right, and much more reliant on Him to get me through these tough times. My kids heard some of those prayers and we learned together how to be more conversational and more personal in our prayers, a practice we all continue today.

My kids saw that I wasn't trying to handle this on my own. I knew I couldn't. They saw how valuable my faith, my family and my friends were. My daughter, in particular, watched and saw how my girlfriends rallied around me. Nearly a year later, she wrote a poem for school about the importance of being a great friend to others and always being there for them. It was beautifully written. It highlighted the deep bonds of friendship that could withstand years and years together. It brought tears to my eyes. Her poem was called "I Am" and included the following lines:

> I pretend to act as if I'm an angel.
> I feel proud when I help a friend out.
> I try to touch many people's hearts.
> I try to be good hearted.
> I hope to be good to everyone I know.
> I am a loving girl who cares about my friends.

I think it's so obvious that I hate to say it here. Clearly you never want to disparage your ex- in front of the kids. He is, after all, their father. No matter how much you might hate him at the moment for what he's done or is doing, never do it. Your kids will remember and I truly believe it will backfire and come back to haunt you or your kids. Imagine the guilt children feel when they are drawn into their parents battling against each other.

As I would meet people whose parents had divorced when they were kids I started asking what got them through it successfully (or not so successfully). Every single one of them credited getting through their parents' divorce successfully because their parents always treated one another with respect, even when they later "discovered" any reasons for their parents' divorce. And, every single one who said that their parents' divorce created havoc and chaos in their lives and impacted them negatively had to deal with feelings of guilt associated with a need to "pick sides" or having to listen to what a "bad person" one of their parents was purported to be.

The state of Georgia requires all people who are getting a divorce who are also parents of children under the age of 18 to attend a four-hour seminar on how to handle the divorce with your children. I sat in the course and felt it was a total waste of time. By this point, this requirement was a final step for most people towards having their divorce granted. Any bad-mouthing of the ex- in front of the children had surely already occurred. I will never forget sitting in this program and listening to the instructors drone on. I'm far too polite, and was sitting far too close to the front, to get out my iPhone® and start playing games or checking email! The instructor said (and this is the honest truth), "For example, you would never want to call your husband a male whore in front of the kids." Were they seriously telling us this? But, when I looked around, it was shocking to see a few people with a clearly shameful look of guilt etched on their face as if to say, "Gulp, oops, shouldn't have said that last week."

Talking about the divorce is something that you will keep discussing with your kids for years to come. Issues which seemed to be OK, may lie dormant and resurface when the kids reach certain developmental stages. Be prepared to continue to discuss, communicate, and share the impact of the divorce. I want my kids to know that it is OK to talk about this. We don't dwell on it. We don't obsess on it. But, we do keep the lines of communication open and I will occasionally do a more "formal" check-in with them to see what's on their minds. Again, communication, talking things out, showing emotions – these are lessons that I want my kids to take with them for the rest of their lives. It may help them in their own relationships in the future.

My kids went through a program called DivorceCare 4 Kids (DC4K™). It was a great program because the kids had peers in the program who were going through the same things they were. We all know how helpful it can be to talk with someone who knows what we are going through. I have seen my kids continue to help other friends and classmates who find themselves in a similar situation. What a blessing if my kids can help others as a result of what they went through. It's not only therapeutic for them, but allows them an opportunity to help someone else. That's a nice side benefit.

Telling your kids will be the hardest thing you ever have to do. Ever. Hopefully this advice will help ease the burden:

Telling your kids

Talk with your husband before you tell the kids about the divorce. For the sake of your children, put aside the hurt and anger you may be feeling, so that you can make decisions together about the details you will need to tell your children. If you don't have this conversation beforehand, you may end up having it in front of your kids, which wouldn't be fair to them. They will surely be left confused and goodness knows there is enough confusion and chaos in this whole situation as it is. Make sure you and your husband are in agreement about what will be said, and don't give the kids "false hope" in an attempt to make this easier for them. This sucks. Trying to make it easier by providing some level of false hope where none exists is cruel.

Deliver the message jointly to the kids. This sends an important message to your kids that you are both capable of working together for their benefit and that you will both continue to be their parents in the future. You will want to tell all of the children at one time. Can you imagine having one of your kids hear it from a sibling? We had the initial discussion all together, then obviously followed up many times with the kids both together and individually. My kids also talked to each other (without either parent) which was amazing. They were able to talk about things and comfort each other.

Remain calm and avoid blaming, yelling or getting angry at the other. This is so critical. Kids hate to see their parents fight in normal day-to-day living, let alone when this kind of news is being shared. The manner in which you present this news to your kids will, in large part, affect the degree of their anxiety and whether they anticipate a positive outcome for themselves. If the meeting becomes a screaming match, your kids will be far more unsettled about what is happening. As a society, we like to know whose "fault" something is, and it's natural to avoid fault and shift blame. Keep these natural tendencies out of the conversation. This should be a "we" conversation – a united front.

Depending on the age of your children, *provide general reasons for what is happening*. It was not important, nor even appropriate, to share the details of what was going on. Instead, we had to provide a more high-level message. The kids wanted to know what was happening, and more specifically, WHY this was happening. Depending on their ages, you will need to have some sort of answer ready that satisfies their curiosity, and frankly, their shock and anger.

Be prepared to provide specific details about the changes your kids can expect. Our kids wanted to know whether we were going to move and whether their dad was moving back to Georgia or staying in Colorado. They wanted to know how they would get to see him and where we would live. You won't necessarily have all these answers settled when you tell them about the divorce, but try to anticipate and have as many answers as possible to give a sense of competence and confidence. Leaving them with a bunch of unanswered questions simply causes more chaos and stress. Help your children to be prepared for these changes by being honest about what you know, and what you don't know.

Outline which parent is leaving the home and where he/she will be living. The more you can tell your kids about where the departing parent will be living and when they will be seeing him or her, the better. They will need to know, right away, that they will be able to maintain a quality relationship with this parent, even though they won't be living under the same roof. In our case, this added a level of complexity because, of course, my ex- had already been living in Colorado for seven months. The kids wanted to know where he would be living on the weekends that he came home to see them.

Reassure the children of your unconditional love ... over and over and over. This was so important in our situation. My children couldn't understand why we were getting a divorce and why the love between mom and dad had "stopped," yet here we were trying to convince them that our love for them would never end (and what's the difference, they were left to wonder?). If they can stop loving each other, can't they stop loving us? My kids were further confused because, like me, they were so blind sided. They both were caught so off-guard. As far as they knew, we were moving in just a few short weeks, yet here we were telling them that instead of moving, we were going to get divorced. It was confusing. Children need lots of reassurance that the divorce is not their fault. We repeatedly told them that nothing they did could have caused, nor prevented, what was happening. In addition, we repeatedly made sure that we were conveying our unconditional love for each of them through both our words and our actions.

Be extra-sensitive, and frankly flexible, in terms of how your kids react to this news. When we told our kids it was so unexpected that we didn't know how they would react. We couldn't predict how they would act or what they would say that day, or for weeks afterwards. Try to be as understanding of no reaction – which is a reaction – as you would be if the children were in tears or extremely angry. Your children may not know how to express their intense emotions appropriately, and it may be some time before they can articulate their feelings. Be patient with them, and be flexible in how you react to how they react. Each of your kids may very well respond differently as well. This is the time for you to demonstrate your parenting flexibility and recognize the differences that your children embrace and demonstrate.

Welcome their questions, encourage their questions, and answer their questions. If your kids are like mine, they will most likely have many questions (which may come tumbling out all at once when you tell them you are getting divorced, or may take longer to formulate and come out over the next few weeks and months). To the extent that you can, be honest and clear in your responses. If you don't know the answer to a question, tell them that. Also, realize that these conversations will unfold in many parts. After you've told the children about the divorce, expect to revisit the topic many times as new questions and concerns arise. I love these follow-up question and answer sessions because I can gauge where the kids are in terms of dealing with the after-shocks and I can see their progress and healing.

Give your kids time to adjust to the news. Please don't expect your kids to "get over this" quickly. On the other hands, kids are re-silient. My kids were out playing with their friends the next day, and to look at them you would think they didn't have a care in the world, but when I asked them if they had told their friends, the answer was no. They were too embarrassed, too ashamed, or too unsure of how to word it. Give them time to deal with this. Help them find the right words. Your kids may need help understanding exactly what to say or how to explain this change in their family to their friends. This is a huge change, and while you may be confident in the hopeful future you envision not only for yourself, but also for them, it will take some time for them to see that future play out. In the meantime, be patient with their needs and make the effort to be a steady presence in their lives. More importantly, if you AREN'T confident (yet) in your own hopeful future, please don't share your own sense of despair with your kids. They need to know that things will get better, and not become bogged down with a sense of your own dread that "life is over."

Bottom line: Telling your kids will be the most difficult thing you ever have to do, but it sets the tone for everything that is going to happen moving forward. Plan it out carefully and deliver the message together.

Putting Your Plan Together:
Things To Think About

"The best thing to give to your enemy is forgiveness; to an opponent, tolerance; to a friend, your heart; to your child, a good example; to a father, deference; to your mother, conduct that will make her proud of you; to yourself, respect."

~ Benjamin Franklin

Once you know, or even strongly suspect, that your marriage is over, you need to start putting together a plan – even if it turns out to simply be a contingency plan. Action is required. Too often, I counsel women who are in denial that this divorce is actually moving forward and consequently they are in a chronic state of inaction, which is the worst place to be. What should the plan entail?

The plan should contain a rough idea of what's at stake. Will you be able to live in the same house? Is there other affordable housing in your area? Will you relocate back "home" or near family, or stay where you are? Will your kids have to change schools? Will they have to drop some extracurricular activities? What are the assets which will need to be split? What are the liabilities that exist? Do you have a job? Do you need a job? What kind of job can you realistically get?

At this point, you don't need to have detailed answers to every question, but you do need to start thinking about these things so as not to be surprised later. One woman I spoke with described a not-so-rare issue given our economy: she and her husband had no assets and a tremendous burden of debt. She explained that she and her soon-to-be-ex-husband would only be splitting debt upon divorce. His job wasn't very steady and so child support and alimony were even questionable. This woman didn't work and hadn't worked outside the home in years. I suggested that she get a job. From the outside looking in, this seemed like a necessity, yet she wasn't yet prepared to look in that mirror.

I counsel women regularly that at some point they need to get "over the shock" of heading for divorce, and instead need to turn to forward-moving, positive action. Now more than ever, your kids need you to help plan for them to ensure that the inevitable disruption that occurs in their lives is minimized. Start thinking about your options. Be smart. Figure things out.

Part of putting together your plan is getting grounded in the details of your financials. My advice? Get grounded in the basics of your financials before a situation exists where you are at the mercy of someone else having to explain it to you. Girlfriends, even in good times, it is irresponsible to not have a general working knowledge of your family income, your expenses, and your investments. I am stunned by the number of women I encounter who have absolutely no clue as to what their household income is, how much they have in investments, or how much they owe. While it's nice to have someone else take care of all these details, it's imperative that both a husband and wife have an operating knowledge of the basics.

I know some happily married couples who review their finances together quarterly to ensure they are aligned and both "in the know." This doesn't have to be a tedious or difficult conversation. It can be fun to jointly review the numbers and know you are on the same page with your spouse about finances and how they are handled in your home. Money is one of the biggest stressors and sources of conflict in a marriage. It pays (pun intended!) to be on the same page.

Unfortunately, I have talked with too many women who have heard the proverbial, "I don't love you anymore" message, and have discovered that while their husbands were coming up with this message, they were also spending all the money. I can't tell you how many times these women have discovered that all the cash has been spent, and that they are on the brink of bankruptcy.

One friend discovered that her husband had been storing away money in private accounts that she didn't have access to during the course of their entire 19 year marriage, as if always planning for something like this. She had never taken the time to pay attention and realize that his take-home pay wasn't adding up.

Another woman told me that her husband had encouraged her to put the title to their house in his name only when they refinanced for "business reasons." She didn't realize that she now had no claim to the property which is where most of their equity was held.

Be smart and always stay involved in your family finances. We don't even have to contemplate the prevalence of divorce to know this is the best thing to do for you and your kids. Think of it another way. I also know a woman whose wonderful husband dropped dead of a heart attack in his early 40's leaving her with three young children. He had taken care of all the family finances, which she truly appreciated at the time, but suddenly she found herself absolutely clueless about what they had and what she needed to take care of herself and her children.

Sadly, many of the women I speak to don't have a solid understanding of their financial picture. I ask, "How much money do you need to pay the bills each month? How much is left over?" and I'm shocked at how many simply can't answer that question. Here is a really simply budget worksheet you can use to get a quick snapshot of where you are at ... and where you may need to cut expenses.

Budget Worksheet

Note: this list isn't designed to be exhaustive, but it will provide a good place to get you started. Be sure to find the monthly cost of all annualized expenses. Consider other monthly expenses you may have that are not reflected on this sheet.

Monthly Income

Total gross monthly income	$
- less taxes, insurance and other payroll deductions)	$
- less savings and contributions to 401(k)	$
TOTAL MONTHLY INCOME	$

Monthly Expenses – Housing Costs

Rent or mortgage	$
Taxes (if not included in mortgage amount)	$
Insurance	$
Electricity	$
Water	$
Gas	$
Garbage/sewer	$
Cable TV	$
Internet service	$
Telephone	$
Home Owners Association	$
Lawn care	$
Alarm service	$
Other housing costs (list)	$
Other	$
Other	$
TOTAL MONTHLY HOUSING EXPENSES	$

Automobile/Vehicle costs (complete separately for each)

Car payment	$
Insurance	$
Auto tags	$
Gasoline	$
Repairs and maintenance	$
Other transportation costs (list)	$
Other	$
Other	$
TOTAL MONTHLY VEHICLE EXPENSES	$

Other Debts (credit card, home equity line, loans)

Creditor 1	$
Creditor 2	$
Creditor 3	$
Creditor 4	$
Creditor 5	$
TOTAL MONTHLY DEBT EXPENSES	$

Children's Expenses

Child care	$
Tutoring	$
Private lessons (music, dance, sports)	$
School tuition	$
Lunch money	$
School supplies and expenses	$
Allowance	$
Clothing	$
Food	$
Medical, Dental, Vision out-of-pocket expenses	$
Personal hygiene and grooming	$

Gifts (from your kids to others)	$
Entertainment and activities	$
Summer camps	$
Other children's expenses	$
Other	$
Other	$
Other	$
Other	$
TOTAL CHILDREN'S EXPENSES	$

Your Expenses

Charitable giving and/or church giving	$
Clothing	$
Food	$
Medical, Dental, Vision out-of-pocket expenses	$
Personal hygiene and grooming	$
Household supplies and products	$
Gifts	$
Entertainment and activities	$
Dry cleaning	$
Recreational expenses (gym membership)	$
Newspaper or magazine subscriptions	$
Cellular telephone	$
Personal education expenses	$
Pet expenses (vet, food, grooming)	$
Other personal expenses	$
Other	$
Other	$
Other	$
TOTAL PERSONAL EXPENSES	$

TOTAL MONTHLY INCOME	$
TOTAL HOUSING EXPENSES	– $
TOTAL VEHCLE EXPENSES	– $
TOTAL CREDITOR EXPENSES	– $
TOTAL CHILDREN'S EXPENSES	– $
TOTAL PERSONAL EXPENSES	– $
MONTHLY INCOME LESS MONTHLY EXPENSES*	$

*Hopefully this number is a positive one and that you don't find yourself "in the red" at the end of each month.

Make a plan ... now! Don't make things worse on you or your children by not doing all you can to be as prepared as possible for all scenarios. It can be utterly overwhelming to think of all the things you need to consider! But, if you take it piece by piece, and one day at a time, it will all come together. I will provide more information in the chapter on partnering with your lawyer on what you will need to think about and what documents you will need to collect.

Bottom line: Invest time now to educate yourself on your financial portfolio. You must have the ability to step back emotionally, and rationally look at what needs to be done from a process and paperwork standpoint. Now more than ever, you need to make sure everything is aligned properly for your kids.

FIGURING IT OUT:
'SOCIAL NETWORKING'
HAS A WHOLE NEW MEANING

*"We must be willing to
get rid of the life we've planned
so as to have the life
that is waiting for us."*

~ Joseph Campbell

As my marriage continued to unravel, I was struck by my ex's inability to explain to me what had gone wrong. In the spirit of taking the high road, I am not going to go into tremendous personal detail here. I will say that my ex- committed adultery, with the girl he dated 20 years earlier, before he and I met. This is not new information. I'm not saying anything that he hasn't shared with others. I'm not saying anything that others hadn't figured out by the time my ex- and his girlfriend got married.

I'm not bitter anymore. I don't consider this acknowledgement to be a deviation from the high road. It is what it is. We've both moved on. In fact, I really like his new wife. My kids love her. I think her boys are precious and her youngest son comes over to play and spend the night regularly. Hating my ex- and hating his wife would do nothing to help the four children involved in this blended family situation. So, yes he cheated on me which is why I feel the need to add information here about how to discover if your husband is having an extra-marital affair.

What I will add is that every single woman I have spoken with who has received the, "I don't love you anymore" speech has asked her husband if there is someone else. And, every single time – yes, every time – the answer has been, "of course not."

And, I'll say this, most women believe it for a while. I don't think they believe it because they really believe it, but because thinking their husbands are capable of cheating on them seems like such a negative thought. And then, at some point, the doubt wins out and the women take some proactive step to "just explore" and see what they can find.

I am amazed by how obvious these men have been in carrying on with their affairs. It makes you want to scream, "What do you think I am, stupid?"

In most instances, a simple check on email, a look at the credit card statements, a glance at the cell phone details, or a look at the frequent flyer accounts is all these women needed to do to confirm their suspicions. In my case, it was a simple $28 charge made on a Tuesday that made me suspicious and started me searching for more.

Everything is electronic these days: everything.

One man told his wife that he was planning a trip to visit his mom (and staying with her), yet a quick check on Hilton.com showed he had made hotel reservations! Was he staying with his mom in a hotel room?

One man told his wife that he was in Chicago for a meeting, and now driving his rental car to Indianapolis for his next meeting. His wife checked Hertz.com the next day and discovered that he had indeed started in Chicago, but had later returned the rental car to Cleveland instead.

One man told his wife he was traveling on business to Palm Springs. She was able to access his airline account. She discovered two reservations made under his name and linked to his account: one for her husband, and one for his secretary!

Cell phone billing is an interesting thing because you not only get to see the destination details, but, more interestingly, you also to get to see the origination details. You can tell where someone is located when they make a call, in addition to the number of the person whom they are calling. This often provides compelling data and helps to fill in the pieces of the puzzle. Most cell phone companies no longer provide paper copies of call details (can you imagine how many trees would be killed to print enough paper to record every phone call we make on our cellular devices?). But, the call-by-call detail is provided electronically in your online account.

The Internet has made it easy to learn about people. A simple Google™ search on an individual can provide a treasure trove of information. See a number on that cell phone bill that you don't recognize? Visit whitepages. com™ and do a reverse look-up. You can input the phone number and usually find the name of the person to whom it is assigned along with an address. From there, you can click on Google Maps™ and usually find a map to the house, and often a photo of the house as well (if it's a land line).

I've spoken with numerous women whose husbands have reconnected with old girlfriends through social media sites like Facebook®, LinkedIn®, or MySpace™ and the ramifications are disastrous. It's always fun to connect with old friends and old flames and see what they are up to, but once you get past the first "hi, how's life treating you" email and the second, "your kids are cute, how did you end up living in Poughkeepsie, where do you work" email, then, really, there is absolutely no need to keep communicating. This is dangerous and I've seen far too often the devastating effects.

Those same social media sites can also be used to find additional data about a person. Divorce records, marriage records, property tax records … it's all there. Have you ever "Googled" yourself? You should try it sometime just to see what's out there.

This section is difficult. There is a fine line between taking the high road and going through the process of discovery to find out what your husband is up to. If you aren't able to get answers directly from your husband about his sudden change in behavior then I am a proponent of being smart and figuring out what you can on your own. You will be better prepared to protect yourself and your children. I'm also a proponent of not over-doing this and becoming suspicious of everything your husband says and does.

Please note the advice provided here is for those women who have a genuine reason to suspect their husband is doing something wrong. I would never advise anyone to "spy" on her husband during the normal course of marriage – ever. That behavior would completely violate that expectation of trust, respect and open communication.

With that caveat being made, there are instances where that "women's intuition" kicks in and we know something is different, that something is wrong, but we can't quite put our finger on it. And, it's not just women suspecting that their husbands are cheating on them. I've spoken with many, many women who suspect their husband has a gambling addiction or is watching Internet porn or taking illegal drugs, or … "fill in the blank." There is something going on which is distracting the husband from focusing on his marriage.

Typically, they have asked their husbands what they are up to, and, of course, the answer is "nothing!" Still, they aren't too sure. They are suspicious, perhaps they have done some sleuthing and have found a phone bill or a receipt that doesn't seem to make sense, and they are not sure what to do next. These women simply want answers. They want to have their concerns alleviated or confirmed, and then they will feel better prepared to deal with the ramifications.

I've passed along this advice several times: pay a little visit to Radio Shack®. Gone are the days of bulky, noisy cassette recorders. For just a few bucks you can purchase a very small digital recorder that can record for over 100 hours without making a sound. You will want to know the law in your state. What you find may or may not be admissible in court if you should want to use it. However, most women I know are simply seeking answers, not seeking proof for the courtroom.

These small digital recorders have provided many an answer. I know a woman who discovered her husband was having an affair because she hid one of these small recording devices under the driver's seat in his car. She heard all of his cell phone conversations with his girlfriend as he drove to and from work every day. He drove a fancy car and used a built-in hands-free system, so she was able to hear both sides of their love affair. Another woman put the recording device in the bottom of a plant pot in their home office. She discovered that her husband was watching internet porn on his work computer at night after she went to bed. So much for his claims that he had to participate on conference calls with their sales offices across the world!

The other industry that is exploding in this day and age is the world of super-sleuth Private Investigators (PI's). Some women I know have insisted upon hiring a private investigator to provide further proof, and confirm once and for all, what it is that their husbands are doing.

There are several things to think about before making that decision. Hiring a PI is a big step … and a costly one. You have to ask yourself why you want to hire a PI. Is it to validate what you already know? Is it just for personal satisfaction? Is it to build a legal case to prove an "at fault" divorce?

Most, if not all PI's, require an up-front retainer fee. This fee is typically $5000. It's amazing how quickly you can burn through that kind of money. Picture having your husband tailed. If it's a stake-out, then certainly one PI will do, but if he's being followed while he drives somewhere, then typically two PI's are used to ensure that they don't lose him in traffic. Now you are paying for not one hourly rate, but two. Most people would have trouble coming up with $5000 that wouldn't be missed from a bank account, or can't imagine putting $5000 on a credit card and expecting it to not be seen. Borrowing $5000 from a family member or a friend is an option, but I don't know too many people whose friends are willing to loan them that kind of money … and there is always the issue of the payback on top of a costly divorce.

It's important to know why you need this information, and how much of it you need. Once you have proof of the behavior occurring, you really don't need more and more proof. Once you have what you need, there is honestly no need for repeated surveillance. It's expensive, and it's painful to see. Why do that to yourself?

The thing to highlight about hiring a PI is to find someone who passes your "gut check." As women, we tend to rely heavily on referrals. We admire someone's hair cut or color and we ask who did it, and then we go see them ourselves. We do this for gynecologists, dentists, babysitters, and the list goes on, don't we? We all operate on referrals, and we all feel better when we hire someone that comes recommended. The same holds true for hiring a PI. On the other hand, be careful about who you share your search for within your network. Asking for a PI referral will draw a lot more buzz than asking for the name of someone's hair stylist!

There are many people out there who hang a shingle and call themselves PI's, but their level of expertise varies greatly. Once you have the name of a PI, make the call and put him or her through a thorough screening process. Ask questions. Determine if this person knows what he is doing. What is his success rate? What is his failure rate (in other words, how often has his cover been blown)? Can he provide an estimate of cost? How does he plan to communicate during the reconnaissance mission? What types of documentation does he provide (video, photos, written report)? Your final decision process should factor in several things: your gut feel, cost, and your perception of his professionalism.

Here's my warning. Using recording devices may be helpful in simply providing some answers to women who have a "gut feel" that something is wrong, and are having trouble figuring it out. Hiring a PI may be necessary if more proof is needed or wanted to firmly establish something. My counsel is to not become so obsessed with finding more and more "dirt" on your husband. There comes a point where you "know what you know," and you have to move on.

Assume you "know what you know." Now what? Whatever the circumstances are surrounding your divorce, it's best to keep them to yourself and a few close confidantes, rather than the public at large. Take the high road!

Why keep quiet? It has nothing to do with protecting your ego. You shouldn't be ashamed to admit that your husband is cheating on you as it's a reflection on him, not you. But there are two other valid reasons for keeping quiet. One, people talk, and they talk in front of their kids, and their kids would hear things and perhaps share them with your kids – and now you have major damage control going on which isn't good for anyone. Two, you really don't want your ex-to find out what you know. By holding your cards close to the vest, you are able to hold onto some ammunition that you might need later.

Yes, it can be really, really tough to keep your mouth shut. One friend said, "I just want to scream at him and confront him, and her, with what I know." Another said, "I had to lie to his mom when she asked me if I thought he was having an affair. Why should I have to lie?" One person said, " I had to endure numerous friends tell me that I was far too smart to not hire a PI and demand to know why I was being so stupid." Yes, it can be painful to stay silent, but one thing I know to be absolutely true, showing restraint and keeping your mouth shut is the best thing you can do.

This is tough. We're talking about needing a tremendous amount of self-control! It gets even harder if your ex- is trying to provoke you and make you angry. He may be doing this to find out what you really know. He may be doing this to make you hate him. After all, if he was successful in making you angry, and then you became a b****, that would suddenly make it easier on him to rationalize what he was doing to end your marriage. Suddenly, it would be very easy for him to twist this around and talk himself into how right he was to treat you this way. Pretty clever, wouldn't you say?

My advice is this: don't feel you have to share what you find – with your husband, or your friends. You should share the information you have if and when you are ready. In the meantime, use it for yourself as you see fit. If you lose your marbles and respond with violent emotion then you take a chance on creating a much more adversarial divorce atmosphere (which isn't good for you or your kids).

And, by keeping your cool as best as you can, you are able to enter the divorce proceedings without this huge cloak of anger and bitterness overshadowing every conversation. If you are like me, you have three main goals as you enter into your divorce proceedings. One, you don't want to be married to this man anymore. Two, you want your kids to come through it unscathed. Three, you want to maintain as much financial security as possible to care for yourself and your kids. Screaming and yelling does not support achieving of any of these three goals. Keeping quiet is difficult. It's hard to know and not say. Definitely harder ... and more worthwhile in the long run. Nobody said that taking the high road would be easy. There are plenty of hazards and potholes and terrifying curves!

Bottom line: Do what you need to do to get your questions answered ... then move on. Don't get bogged down in the details, and think long and hard about what you are going to share with others. Showing restraint is part of the high road.

INTERPRETING THE SIGNS:
SHOULD I BE WORRIED?

*"Respect is love
in plain clothes ...
and the first duty
of love is to listen."*

~ Frankie Byrne

People often ask me, "Did you know he was having an affair?" As you already know, I had no idea. They then will ask, "But didn't you see any signs?"

In hindsight, yes, there were lots of signs, or perhaps better said, lots of things that just struck me as "odd." When I put them all in black and white in the pages of this book, I can't help but think how stupid I was. But, at the time, I didn't stop to think about them all and add up the weight of their totality. In this hectic and crazy pace in which we exist, how often do you take the time to stop and think and connect all the dots? We need to do more of this. We need to be more aware. Instead, I think we often get caught up in the whirlwind of work, raising kids, volunteering, exercising, cooking, cleaning, taking care of our parents, hanging out with our friends, chauffeuring our kids around, until we fall in bed each night just exhausted ... and with no time to think and reflect.

It seems people have their own stories for how they discovered their husband was having an affair. One friend's husband was a consultant on assignment in Orlando. Poor thing. He led the typical consulting lifestyle and flew out every Monday morning and returned home every Thursday night just exhausted from such a long week at work. One weekend, they planned for she and the kids to meet him in Orlando to spend a few days at Disney World®. They landed and drove to his corporate apartment. The kids were hungry and she opened the refrigerator to see what she could find to feed them. Funny thing ... there was an open gallon of orange juice in the fridge. Even funnier ... none of them (neither she, nor he, nor their kids) ever drank orange juice. Ever! Makes you want to ask, "What do you think I am, Stupid?"

Another friend was on vacation in San Francisco with her parents, her husband, and their two children. About a year earlier, her husband admitted to having an affair with a woman who lived in Sacramento. They worked through it and were now enjoying a nice family vacation together. While on vacation, her husband announced that he had to leave to attend an urgent meeting in Los Angeles the next day. Oh, by the way, this meeting was going to be held on the day before a holiday weekend when most people weren't even working. He left for the meeting then "got sick" while driving to Los Angeles and ended up spending the night near Sacramento. For you readers that don't know your U.S. geography very well, you would never drive near Sacramento on your way from San Francisco to Los Angeles. Makes you want to ask, "What do you think I am, Stupid?"

Another woman came to the realization that her husband never parted ways with his BlackBerry.® Never. She began watching and realized that he put it next to the bed at night. Took it into the bathroom with him. Laid it next to the shower. It was literally always at his side. In the past, he would plug it in to charge on the kitchen counter or leave it on the table when he would go out for a run. One day, he left it sitting on the counter while he went upstairs to grab his shoes. Serendipitously, a text chime sounded and she glanced at his BlackBerry®. The graphic message made her turn red ... with anger. Makes you want to ask, "What do you think I am, Stupid?"

Given the prevalence of infidelity in this country, it's no surprise that article after article exists with titles like, "How to Tell Your Husband is Cheating on You," or "The Top Ten Signs He is Having an Affair." I read a lot of these articles post-divorce. Perhaps I should have read them earlier, but I never read these articles because I honestly never thought they would pertain to me. Why would I read an article on how to pilot an airplane if I have no intention of ever actually being a pilot? Why read these articles, I would think when I passed them in a magazine, when I didn't think my husband would ever cheat on me?

I would love to give proper credit to the authors of all the articles I read "after the fact," but at this point, they appear in my brain as just a series of points that I remember.

I read many articles that claimed to identify what makes a man cheat on his wife. Hmm ... I wonder if we could use this almost like an indicator pre-marriage of whether a person has a predisposition towards being unfaithful? Now there's a quiz that every new girlfriend should give her boyfriend as they start to get serious.

Determining the Possibility

What would you circle in response to these questions?

YES / NO Is your husband "just good friends" with people of the opposite sex? Does he talk about a certain friend who is a woman more than others?

Before you know it, that friendship connects on a deeper level and morphs into "friends with benefits" status.

YES / NO Does your husband thrive on adventure sports? Does he relish being reckless and "living life on the edge?"

Some men truly thrive on the suspense and the deception that goes along with an affair as much as the suspense and the adrenalin rush from participating in adventure sports. There is an element of danger (Will I be caught?) and an element of winning (I got away with it again!) that many men enjoy.

YES / NO Did your husband have a great deal of sex before marriage?

If he is used to having a lot of sex with a lot of different women, then perhaps the idea of becoming faithful and monogamous "until death do us part" may not be something he is willing to do. If he was a player before marriage, he will probably be a player after marriage.

YES / NO Did your husband cheat in previous relationships?

If he cheated once, he'll probably cheat again. Enough said.

YES / NO Does your husband have friends who have cheated on their spouses?

How many times did your parents caution you to choose your friends wisely? How many times have you encouraged your kids to be careful who they hang around with? The same holds true for us as adults. Surround yourself with wise people, and you will be wise, but surround yourself with fools and you will get hurt. That's actually from the Bible. Proverbs 13:20 says, "Whoever walks with wise people will be wise, but whoever associates with fools will suffer harm." Peer pressure is very much alive and well. If your husband is hanging around friends who have cheated on their wives, it may only be a matter of time before he joins in as well! If he sees them getting away with it, why not join in?

YES / NO   Is your husband connected in his faith?

I firmly believe that a strong path helps to at least provide guardrails for living life and knowing when an actionable decision is going to cross the ethical line he has drawn for himself. Pay attention to your husband if his faith, while historically important, suddenly stops being a priority.

I recall reading another article that spoke about why men are unfaithful. Interesting, I thought. Can we really rationalize an explanation as to why men break their covenant of marriage and cheat? I was skeptical, but read the article. I seem to recall there being a few different categories that were highlighted.

One was the "see-if" affair where a man has an affair just to "see-if" things truly would be greener on the other side of the fence or to "see-if" what they think is missing from their relationship truly is. There was also a category called "sexual-panic." This kind of cheating was characterized by a husband starting to feel less desirous of his wife and starting to panic that his sexual desire was dissipating, so what better way to prove his own masculinity than to go out and prove he could still get it up. Nice.

The one that struck a chord with me, however, was the "I just want out of this marriage, but I don't have the guts to tell her" kind of cheating. The author called this the "ejector-seat" affair. These kinds of affairs clearly create the exit strategy which the man is seeking, albeit they are not the kindest or the most honest way of going about things.

I decided to do some research into the prevalence of adultery. Here's what I found. It's shocking to me (still!). According to Maggie Scarf, author of *Intimate Partners*, first published in 1987 by Random House, re-issued in 1996 by Ballentine, "Most experts do consider the 'educated guess' that at the present time some 50 to 65 percent of husbands and 45 to 55 percent of wives become extramaritally involved by the age of 40 to be a relatively sound and reasonable one."

According to Peggy Vaughan, author of *The Monogamy Myth*, first published in 1989 by Newmarket Press (third edition published 2003), "Conservative estimates are that 60 percent of men and 40 percent of women will have an extramarital affair. These figures are even more significant when we consider the total number of marriages involved, since it's unlikely that all the men and women having affairs happen to be married to each other."

And, if this wasn't shocking and depressing enough, some more recent statistics are beginning to show that up to 80% of marriages will at some time struggle with the challenge of infidelity. When you add in emotional affairs and internet affairs, it rises to 90%! Unbelievable!

Back to the initial question and how we began this chapter. What are some signs to look for in determining if your husband is having an affair? We already went through the Midlife Crisis quiz of indicators that your husband may be "prone" to having a crisis. This list is more specific. This list highlights the signs that he may actually be having a midlife crisis at this moment! How's this for a Top Ten list?!

Top Ten Signs of a Current Midlife Crisis

1. He has a sudden concern with how he dresses … he buys new clothes that wouldn't typically be his style … he invests in new underwear.

2. He has a new interest in working out and eating healthy … new concern about how his body looks … perhaps he starts to lose weight … perhaps he gets a new haircut or starts wearing new cologne … he checks himself for bad breath.

3. He suddenly has business meetings late at night or an increase in the number of business trips he must take … he has unexplained times away from home or unusual demands on his time.

4. He is suddenly tied to his cell phone … never leaving it unattended … there are secret phone calls or lots of wrong numbers … he begins to speak in hushed tones or goes outside to answer his calls … he changes the amount of time he spends talking on the phone, texting, or sending emails.

5. He begins talking a lot about another person … this is often the beginning of the emotional affair where nothing has happened yet, but he's becoming obsessed with thinking and talking about her.

6. He becomes secretive about his cell phone bills or his credit card charges ... he hides or "loses" receipts.

7. He becomes interested in new behaviors ... and often changes his likes and dislikes as it pertains to sex.

8. He is unavailable for extended periods of time, when ordinarily you could always reach him ... and when you ask where he was, you get a random, nebulous response.

9. He changes his communication habits ... suddenly becoming overly detailed, or overly evasive and private.

10. He starts acting distant and seems pre-occupied and says things like: "It's nothing about you, it's just that I'm unhappy. There is really nothing you can do to help or change it. It feels as if we are more like roommates than spouses. I don't feel 'in love' with you anymore. You don't seem like my soul-mate and that is really what I want in my life."

I think it goes without saying that you can't be paranoid about the items listed above and freak out every time your husband gets a haircut or doesn't answer his cell phone. The message is clearly not to become suspicious and create doubt or insecurities in your marriage. That certainly isn't healthy. Lists like this are like stereotypes. They help us to identify and perhaps know what to expect from certain things, but we always have to be willing to look for the differences and the individual circumstances which make this "different than" the norm.

It's about staying checked-in on your relationship and keeping your radar on for changes that things just feel "odd" or "different." After a few patterns of "hmm... that doesn't feel quite right" you may want to start to pay more attention.

Bottom line: It can happen to you. Stay alert. Read the signs and never lose sight of the big picture of your marriage. This is not a place for complacency. Keep the lines of communication open at all times.

LEANING ON YOUR SUPPORT NETWORK: FRIENDS AND MANY OTHERS!

*"Life isn't about waiting
for the storm to pass ...
it's about learning to
dance in the rain."*

~ Anonymous

Throughout that dreadful season of my life, my girlfriends were amazing. Their husbands were amazing. I would never have gotten through all of this without them. I know that for a fact. They took care of me and the kids. They made us feel normal. They allowed us to laugh and to cry. In their own way, each person did something unique and special for us.

One Thursday night, one of my girlfriends invited several of us over. We sat on her back porch, ate dessert, and talked, and talked and talked. I was beat. I looked like hell. That was a really bad night, and I knew my friends were worried about me. But, they didn't tell me I looked like hell. They didn't tell me I looked beat. Instead, they filled several hours with conversation until finally I knew it was time to go home. I knew I would be able to fall asleep. I sent the following email the next morning:

> *There hasn't been a day that has gone by in the last few months that I haven't thanked God for my amazing friends. I would not be getting through this if it weren't for all of you. I feel your prayers, your love, and your support more than you know and it is truly sustaining me. I wouldn't wish this on my worst enemy, but with my faith, my family and my friends, I will get through this. Thanks for all you guys are doing. Thanks for last night – it felt good to laugh. I love you, Monique*

Moral of the story: rely on your friends. Count on them! Treasure them. And, if you are the friend of someone going through something like this right now, don't underestimate the power of your interaction. My friends took the kids and me out to eat. They invited us over. They sent me cards. One friend sent me a card every couple of days. Some were funny, some were cute, some were serious ... and all meant the world to me. Some friends took my kids so I could have free time to try and figure things out. Others stopped by with a Starbucks®, or would encourage me to meet them there. Others brought me books filled with wisdom. Some brought flowers. Some brought little trinkets with reminders about Faith and Family. Every single thing they did meant the world to me.

Think about when someone you love is hurting. You want to help them, right? You want to do something grand to take away the pain. Yet often, there is nothing on a grand scale that can be done. We can't take away their pain. But, the little things count just as much. It's incredible how much those little things can add up and help out. So often we think there is nothing we can do, and so often we are wrong! If you know of someone going through a situation like this, be there for her. In whatever form or fashion that takes for you, be there. And, be there repeatedly, not just once or twice. It's like when someone dies. Everyone is there for you in the beginning, but as the months go by, everyone returns to their normal day to day lives and tends to forget that you may still be in pain and grieving. Stay in tune and stay connected.

Find your support group. Find that group of people whom you trust, who will give you good advice, who will be there when you need a shoulder to cry on and who will indulge you when it's time for you to laugh. There are many different "sources" of support groups.

I believe that as a woman I can have many best friends. I don't subscribe to the "one best friend theory." By this age, I have many different best friends who each add their own value to different situations. I'm not sure who wrote this, but in different iterations it can found in many different places. It rings true for me.

> When I was little, I used to believe in the concept of one best friend, and then I started to become a woman. And then I found out that if you allow your heart to open up, God would show you the best in many friends. One friend's best is needed when you're going through things with your man. Another friend's best is needed when you're going through things with your Mom. Another when you want to shop, share, heal, hurt, joke, or just "be." One friend will say let's pray together, another let's cry together, another let's laugh together, another let's walk together. One friend will meet your spiritual need, another your shopping fetish, another your love for movies, another will be with you in your season of confusion, another will be your clarifier, another "the wind beneath your wings." But whatever their assignment in your life, on whatever the occasion, on whatever the day, or wherever you need them to meet you with their gym shoes on and hair pulled back or to hold you back from making a complete fool of yourself...those are your "best" friends. It may all be wrapped up in one woman, but for many, it's wrapped up in several ... one from 7th grade, one from high school, several from the college years, a couple from old jobs, several from church, on some days your mother, on some days your daughters, others your sisters, and on some days it's the one that you needed just for that day or week that you needed someone with a fresh perspective, or the one who didn't know all our "baggage," or the one who would just listen without judging...those are "good girlfriends /best friends."

You will benefit from having a diverse support network. Don't place all your need for support on one person. It's not fair to her, nor to you. I found that different friends offered different levels of support. Some had been through this themselves and provided a perspective that not everyone else could. Others provided great support based on faith and prayer. Others provided support by making me laugh. Others listened to me when I dropped the F-bomb. My family was a wonderful support. My mom never stopped listening to my updates. She wasn't judgmental. My brother made it a habit to call me every few days just to check on his little sister. My minister provided the listening ear and the sound advice I needed to hear, along with a really good dose of humor!

It's amazing how your friends, and your support group at large, will rally around you in your time of crisis. This is my personal Top Ten list of things my friends did for me for which I will forever be grateful:

Top Ten Friend Moments

1. Helping with my kids … by inviting the kids to their homes and giving me some time to be alone.

2. Providing a listening ear … by knowing when I wanted to talk about what I was going through, and when I wanted to escape from it.

3. Caring for me … by giving me food, cards, books, trinkets and tokens of their love that I could carry with me to remember I wasn't alone.

4. Checking in on me frequently … through a quick email here, a voice mail message, or simply stopping by because they were "in the area."

5. Accepting me for all I was going through … they didn't judge me; they didn't lecture me (too much) for losing weight or dropping the F-bomb; they knew the real me would return in time when the healing began.

6. Choosing sides … they (whoever "they" is) say never to choose sides during a divorce, but my friends showed me incredible loyalty which is so appreciated.

7. Trying to understand … even if they didn't know why I couldn't share everything with them about what I was going through. They were patient. There is a time to share and a time to talk … some friends are

easier to talk to about some things than others. Sometimes it's easier to share intimate things with total strangers. Don't judge the timing of what is shared. Don't take it personally.

8. Including me ... by not making me feel like a 5th wheel and continuing to invite me to all the normal couples things I would have attended in the past with my ex- ... and they acted like it was no big deal!

9. Making me feel loved, beautiful, needed and wanted and just generally helping to keep my self-esteem where it needed to be!

10. Praying for me ... both with me and during their own prayer time ... and I felt each and every one of those prayers.

I am also a big fan of your support network taking on a professional edge as well. Clearly, I connected with my minister early on in this process, and I also started to see a marriage counselor. As I mentioned in an earlier chapter, one great step I took which I can't emphasize enough was joining a group called DivorceCare™ I signed my kids up for the companion group called DivorceCare For Kids™ (DC4K™, www.dc4k.org). These two programs provide a divorce recovery support group to help adults and children (ages 5-12) heal from the process of going through divorce. I can't say enough good things about this program. We met weekly for 13 weeks. We dealt with every emotion of going through a divorce. Our program facilitators were amazing and gave us great hope that we would indeed get through this.

When I first started to attend, I went in with the attitude that I probably wasn't going to get much out of the program because I already had such a great support group with my friends. However, I couldn't very well ask my kids to attend the program without me role modeling my attendance as well.

It turns out, I was wrong. I got so much out of the program, by being surrounded by a small group of peers who were going through the same exact thing I was at that very moment. We were able to share resources, share ideas, and "support" one another. It was terrific!

I can't say enough about how great the DC4K™ program was for my kids. They really got a lot out of it and I wonder how well they would have dealt with all of this without that support group of other boys and girls going through a similar situation. They learned that it's OK to rely on others and share your personal thoughts. They learned what is "normal" to feel when your parents get divorced, and more importantly, they learned to verbalize those feelings.

My personal support group grew to include my lawyer, my accountant, my financial planner, my gynecologist, and the list goes on and on. Think about it: each of these people had a reason to know what was going on in my life to help protect me in one way or another. I carefully reached out to each person, filled them in on the high-level details, and together we figured out how best they and their respective professions could support the kids and me through the divorce.

Most of the professions in my support network outlined above probably make sense. If you are like most women, you probably paused or hesitated when you read "gynecologist." Think about it. If you even suspect your husband may have been unfaithful, you have to get checked out. Remember all those lectures given in high school and college about when you sleep with one person you are really sleeping with all the people they have ever slept with … and that their partners have ever slept with, and on and on.

Let me tell you, that was an embarrassing and awkward day. I've had the same gynecologist for nearly eight years. I see her once a year for my annual exam. We say hello, catch up on the small talk, she does her "thing" from a medical perspective, I get dressed, and I tell her I'll see her again in 365 days. That's the way it's always been – until this time. When I called to book my appointment, I was three months ahead of schedule. When I booked the appointment, the front desk receptionist asked what I needed to come in for. I told her it was for my annual exam. She responded that I didn't need to be seen for three more months. "I know," I said, "but I just really need to get in to see Dr. Sonso." She insisted upon putting a "reason for visit" in the appointment book. I think I mumbled something about wanting to get tested for sexually transmitted diseases (STDs). That seemed to satisfy her. It humiliated me.

It's embarrassing to have to go the gynecologist and ask for these tests to be done. Several women have told me they would rather ignore the chance that they might have an STD rather than have to go tell a professional that their husband was unfaithful and ask to have these tests run. Don't be crazy! Ignorance is not bliss.

I was fortunate that I had seen the same gynecologist for so many years and had built somewhat of a relationship with her. Once I got past making the appointment and figuring out what to say to the receptionist, I had no trouble sharing with my doctor what was going on. I insisted on having every test in the book. But, when she sent me to the lab and the lab technician was looking at the lab sheet to see what tests had been ordered, that's when the embarrassment kicked in. It was clear to see that the blood tests that were being ordered had everything to do with every kind of STD known. I wonder what the lab technician thought? It was horrible. I felt filthy. No one should feel that way.

Oh, and by the way, it wasn't just one round of blood tests. My gynecologist suggested a second round of blood tests to be performed three months later to make sure nothing was lying dormant and would later pop up. So three months later, I endured the same humiliation again when I entered the lab and handed the lab tech the order sheet!

Unfortunately, there is one other area of support that I need to mention. Many women have told me that they have become fearful of their husbands as their marriages have unraveled. It's a puzzling dichotomy. To go from fully trusting someone and thinking you know who you are married to, to wondering who this person is who is often times demonstrating absurd and erratic behavior, can be troubling, and frankly, quite frightening.

These fears are real. People do crazy things when they feel they are backed into a corner, and often times the reality of divorce, of being "found out," of losing assets or a certain lifestyle, drives people to do things that seem out of character. Nobody wants to become the star of a Lifetime Movie of the Week about a distressed husband who took things too far.

My advice is always the same. Trust your intuition. If you suspect something isn't right and that behavior may be crossing the line, don't intentionally provoke any anger or rage. Leave the situation immediately, and take your kids. More than once, I have counseled women to call the local authorities to provide them with an alert as to what is going on. Change your locks if you can. Have a security system installed. Do what your gut tells you to do to protect yourself and your children.

Most importantly, don't keep your fears to yourself. It's not shameful or embarrassing. It's reality. Share your concerns with your support group, and they can help keep an eye on things.

Your Professional Support Group Contact List

(assuming you know the numbers for your mom and your best friends by heart,
here are some other numbers you may want to keep handy)

Resource	Contact Name	Phone Number
Accountant		
Divorce Attorney		
Divorce Care Program/ Therapist		
Financial Planner		
Gynecologist		
Minister / Rabbi		
Police Dept (if needed)		
Other		

Bottom line: Don't try to go through life alone. People want to help –
let them! Different people will add value at different parts of this season in
life. You have to trust that they have your best interests at heart.

Managing Your Vices:
Skinny and Sad, or Fat and Happy?

"A healthy body
and soul come from
an unencumbered
mind and body."

~ Ymber Delecto

I had some really rough months. I was moving forward with the divorce process. I was sad. I was mad. I wasn't eating. My "vice" turned to over-exercising and drinking Starbucks®. I was an over-caffeinated, high-energy, angry woman. I had adrenalin flowing through my system like blood. I was wired up and fired up! I was a Starbucks®-drinking, exercising fool who had a mouth like a sailor.

I became the Atlanta version of those Hollywood types you see who never appear in *People Magazine* without a Starbucks® in hand. I rarely drank coffee before this. Now, however, Starbucks® should be thanking me for single handedly doing my part to help them through their tough economic times. When most people in this world were thinking $4 is too much for a cup of coffee, I was going there twice a day. I had frequented Starbucks® less than a dozen times in my life (always opting for a hot tea option), but suddenly Iced Coffee was my daily drink of choice.

My other vice was over-exercising. I was angry and needed an outlet for my energy. I would go for long walks. I would get on the elliptical for over an hour at a time. I had always been healthy and exercised to stay fit, but exercise took on a new meaning by serving as an outlet for my emotions and helping me to keep my sanity. It felt good to exercise and work up a good sweat. I could put on my headphones and get lost in my music.

We turn to "vices" to get through times of stress. I have spoken with several women who turned to alcohol to deal with their pain. This is a dangerous vice for so many obvious reasons. One woman had turned to over-eating to deal with her depression and was now unhappy with her life, and with her body. Unfortunately, another woman I spoke with had become obsessed with proving she "still had it" and would go out and hook up with a different man as often as she could. She said that it felt good to know that someone still found her desirable, but she admitted that she always felt empty and alone at the end of the night. Obviously many vices require the intervention of a professional counselor, and I encourage anyone who feels that her "vice" has gotten out of control to seek professional help as soon as possible ... if not for you, then for the welfare of your children.

I think women often turn to vices to help them feel like they can control something. Her marriage may be crumbling out of control, and she may feel like she can't do anything to make it stop, but she can control how much she eats, or doesn't eat, or how much she exercises, or how many new clothes she buys.

I've heard women lament that they must have done something "wrong" in order for their husbands to leave them. Stop this train of thought! Don't go there. It's not healthy to venture into the world of, "If only ..." If only I was smarter, or skinnier, or prettier, or a better cook, or better in bed, or whatever. Don't go to "shoulda-coulda-woulda." I should have ..." dressed differently, laughed more, nagged less, wore more make-up, or whatever. Don't "should" on yourself.

My vice was Starbucks® and exercise. I'm thankful for those vices. I know they could have been worse. But even those, when taken to excess, can be dangerous. Needless to say, drinking coffee and exercising over-stimulated my system and I lost a lot of weight. Most people would probably love this, but losing a lot of weight through a vice can be just as bad as drinking too much or overeating. My friends were worried about me. I just didn't have an appetite, and what I was eating, I was quickly working off at the gym.

Rest assured, I'm now back to my normal weight. On the light side, it was fun buying some new clothes, but I have to admit, looking back at the photos, I was too skinny and it showed. My face was gaunt and hollow. I looked horrible.

Later, when I reached my forgiveness stage (stay tuned for that amazing transformation) and started eating again (and gaining weight), I, of course, lamented the pounds I was putting back on. My dear friend Michelle asked me, "Would you rather be skinny and sad, or fat and happy?" How appropriate! I burst out laughing knowing I would much rather be happy then endure another season like the one I had just gone through!

Bottom line: Vices! People turn to them to get through stressful times. At the end of the day, watch out for your vices and make sure they aren't inhibiting your ability to stay on the high road.

Using the "F" Word:
The Power of Forgiveness

"The weak can never forgive.
Forgiveness is the attribute of the strong."

~ Mahatma Gandhi

"There is no revenge so
complete as forgiveness."

~ Josh Billings

"It's simple: when you haven't forgiven
those who've hurt you, you turn your back
against your future. When you do forgive,
you start walking forward."

~ Tyler Perry

This may well be the most important chapter in this book. If you hear nothing else, hear this!

I don't typically talk like a sailor. I don't frequently use cuss words (as my kids call them), but somehow the summer of "The Pronouncement," I was dropping the F-bomb a fair bit. I was mad. I'm not one to kick walls or throw punches. I don't swing golf clubs. I don't scratch the paint off shiny new red cars. I don't throw things on the front lawn. Swearing became my way of showing anger. I was pissed off, angry, furious, and it showed in my language. F-this. F-that. F-him. I hated it. I felt like I was giving a bit of who I am away every time I said it. My friends commented on my new choice of words. They acknowledged that this wasn't me.

You know what? I soon discovered a much more powerful F-word. Forgiveness. It's absolutely magical. It's selfish as all get-out. It's life changing. Forgiveness is the most powerful thing you can do for YOURSELF.

Ultimately, I reached a tipping point. The anger was getting old. I was tired of being consumed with negative thoughts. I am not a nasty person by nature, and this was taking its toll on me.

I had gone to the lake, and it was a fabulous weekend. It was the kids and me, and then two of my friends, their husbands, and their kids. There were five adults, and seven kids. We played on the water for hours, we ate great food, we laughed, and we worked and cleaned! What? Worked and cleaned?

My friends were absolutely amazing and out of the goodness of their hearts they sacrificed part of their fun Labor Day weekend to help me get the lake house back in shape both inside and outside. My friends pulled weeds, trimmed bushes, laid pine bark, deep cleaned the entire inside of the house, changed out filters, replaced light bulbs, fixed doors, and on and on!

I was incredibly thankful. It was during this weekend that I realized that all my anger was only hurting me and my kids. It wasn't hurting my ex-. He wasn't feeling the brunt of my anger. He didn't see me plotting revenge on the elliptical every day. He wasn't having his blood pressure go sky high thinking about what was going on.

I was pulling weeds in the front yard, watching some of my friends lay pine bark, while others started fixing dinner. I was watching the kids run around the yard, and suddenly, I realized that I needed to forgive my ex-. My friend Michelle had given me a sign that read, "Let Go and Let God" that I had displayed in my kitchen. I finally understood what that meant. I had to let go … and let God take over. I won't say I experienced instantaneous peace, but I did have a very calm, rational feeling that it was time for me to let go of the hurt and the anger and forgive him. Ultimately, it was life-changing … for me and my kids.

Within a week of deciding to forgive my ex-, I had several different people mention to me how happy and at peace I looked. Clearly with the anger gone, I did have a different look about me. While I felt it internally, I was absolutely amazed that it was noticeable physically as well.

Ironically, I had several friends get "mad" at me when I told them I had forgiven my ex-. They expressed surprise and concern that I was able to forgive him and worried that this might mean I wouldn't be "smart" negotiating our settlement. What they didn't realize is how selfish an act it is to forgive someone. Forgiveness is unilateral. It only has to do with you, the person doing the forgiving, and has nothing to do with the person who is being forgiven. It doesn't mean you won't hold that person accountable. It doesn't mean what they did is erased. It doesn't mean there won't be consequences for their actions. It does mean that I am not going to waste any more of my emotional energy consumed by what someone else did. Forgiveness allowed me to go from hate and anger, to an attitude of "whatever." Seriously, just "whatever." Do you know how liberating that can be?

I realized this: forgiveness is selfish. I decided to let go of the anger. I decided to forgive my ex-. I felt much better. It was all about me. It was a revolutionary thought and I loved it. Forgiveness was amazing. It was the best I had felt in ages. My friend Allis shared this quote with me and it hit me like a ton of bricks:

Peace: it doesn't mean to be in a place where there is no noise, trouble or hard work. It means to be in the midst of all those things and still be calm in your heart!

~ *Author Unknown*

Once I forgave my ex-, I felt truly at peace. Sure, my situation still sucked … big time, but I was no longer harboring such a vicious anger in my heart. I was no longer planning my revenge. In the midst of all the noise, the trouble and the hard work, I was calm in my heart.

My minister commented one night at church about how different I looked. He said he sensed a new peace about me and asked what was going on. I told him I had forgiven my ex- and I asked him why more people didn't choose forgiveness instead of holding onto grudges. I've seen people hold a grudge for years, and all it does is hurt the person holding the grudge. If they had forgiven years earlier and moved on, everyone would have been happier.

My mom and my friends were still not sure about this new forgiveness thing. They were still angry with my ex- and found it surprising when I decided to let go of my anger. The general consensus seemed to be that by forgiving him, I was going to let him off the hook. They were concerned that I was going to give in to his demands in the divorce. I assured them that there was no correlation between forgiving someone, and holding that same person accountable for their actions. Just because I forgave him, doesn't mean I was going to let him walk all over me. Just because I forgave him, doesn't mean I wasn't going to hold him accountable. What it did mean was that I was not going to spend hours each day thinking negative energy-draining thoughts about him. I was not going to ruin my health by holding all these pent-up emotions inside. I was not going to waste any more negative energy on this.

In fact, I argued to my mom and my friends, by forgiving him I was now able to negotiate from a position of power. It wasn't just emotional anymore. Instead, I was also able to see things a bit more rationally and that made all the sense in the world.

Please take away this message: choosing to forgive is the single most powerful thing you can do for you and your kids. It is life changing. It is selfish (and that is OK!). If you are still struggling with this concept of forgiveness, then read this portion again and again and again. Forgiveness is the single most important thing you can do for yourself and your children.

I had a great conversation with a friend about my opinion that giving forgiveness is a selfish act. He argued that forgiveness is not really a selfish act, but instead a communal act. We got into all sorts of dialogue and debated the essence of forgiveness. His point was that forgiveness builds community. Because of my decision to forgive my ex-, I was able to lay the foundation towards building a relationship of community between us, between his wife and me, amongst all our children, amongst our friends, etc. Without forgiveness, that community and those relationships wouldn't have been possible.

At the end of the day, I believe both points are valid. Making the decision to forgive is truly all in your hands, which I believe makes it a selfish act, but the results of that forgiveness are more communal in nature since the ripple effect extends so far beyond just you.

I am certainly not an expert on forgiveness, but I do believe that you have to go through a certain number of natural responses before you are able to truly forgive and mean it genuinely. Like Kübler-Ross' stages of grief that I learned about in 10th grade psychology, so too do I believe that there are certain stages that you have to go through in a situation like this.

I also firmly believe that everyone will go through those stages in their own time. Don't let anyone else dictate how long you should be in denial, or how long you should be in anger, or how long you should grieve. You alone will know when you are ready to continue with your healing and move on to the next phase. Some people are able to move through them more quickly than others. And when you reach the phase that forgiveness seems like the next best choice for you, take it, do it, and rejoice in it!

I've had women say to me, "I don't think I'll ever get to forgiveness. I'm still so angry. I hate him." And, as our conversation continues, I start to see the rolling tide of thoughts and feelings and anger begin to overwhelm her, then her eyes tear up, and her voice starts to shake, and I can tell her blood pressure has sky-rocketed again and she's back in the moment of hate. This tide ebbs and flows every day. Sound familiar?

Women know when they are going there, when they are getting sucked back in with that emotional tidal wave again. My advice? Find a mantra, a verse, or a quote, and every time you feel yourself being dragged to that negative place, just silently repeat it to yourself. I had a necklace I wore almost every day, and every time I would start to feel dragged under, I would reach for my necklace and say, "Patience, Strength, Faith." One woman I know says, "Inner Peace is Good," over and over again until the anger dissipates. Find a technique that works for you, and it will become easier and easier to release the negativity when it surfaces.

I know my children noticed my transformation when I chose to let go of the anger and forgive my ex-. I did have a new peace about me and it showed.

I am repeatedly asked, "Please teach me how to forgive." I don't know how to do that. I wish I did. I want everyone to feel the liberation and peace that comes with forgiveness. I tell women that it will happen if they are open to dropping some of the anger and looking forward to the future, instead of dwelling on the past.

I think I was able to find forgiveness by focusing on the positive. I had to believe that my ex- had lost who he was somewhere in the midst of all this. He had become a different person and certainly not the man I married. I didn't want to think that this was his true character. Instead, I believe that he lost his way and totally veered off course for a while. I think he allowed himself to compromise his belief system and that he forced himself to rationalize his behavior. It's sad for me to think about because this "season" will always be a part of his life. I began to pray for my ex-. I believe focusing on the future, and hoping my ex- would find his way back (for the good of our children), helped me to find forgiveness.

Ironically, it was during this time of discovering the power of forgiveness that I came across the following quote. It summed up my new outlook just perfectly. It became my new mantra. To this day, I have it prominently displayed in my house where I can see it every day and be reminded that this is how I want to live my life.

Live purposefully. Think rightly.
Serve generously. Forgive quickly.

Bottom line: Forgiveness is the ultimate goal. It is simultaneously a very selfish act and a very communal act in that it builds relationships you have yet to even see. Forgiveness brings you peace and it helps you move on. Find it in your heart to honestly forgive. You will be glad you did.

Partnering with an Attorney:
You Can't Do This on Your Own

*"All the events of your life
are there because you have
drawn them there.
What you choose
to do with them
is up to you."*

~ Richard Bach

My friends will tell you that I am a very decisive person. When action needs to be taken, I'm not one to procrastinate. And, this situation was no different. Once I knew that any hope for reconciliation was over, I was done. I took proactive steps to move forward, and I went to see a divorce attorney.

It's important to recognize that everyone reaches their threshold at different times. Some women stay with a husband who clearly doesn't want to be in the marriage for months, even years, in hopes of reconciling. Some women give a tremendous number of "second chances." I've seen it all. It varies depending on the person and the situation and there is no one right answer. There is no perfect timing or perfect plan, and nobody can tell you what is right for you. Only you will know when the marriage is over.

Everyone will reach their saturation point at different times. For one woman, that moment came with the realization that she is not being much of a role model to her daughter by staying in a loveless marriage. For another woman, that moment came when she finally reached her own conclusion that even though her husband claimed to love her with all his heart, and begged for her forgiveness, he had a pattern of engaging in behaviors that were destructive to their marriage. It took her a while to reach that point. Her friends and family had all reached that point months earlier and were incredibly frustrated that she "couldn't see it." When the timing was right for her though, she did see it, and she moved on appropriately.

I actually received flack from some people who thought I had consulted a divorce attorney too quickly. I promised myself early on that I would give 100% towards making my marriage work, but when I knew it was over, I would move forward to ending that chapter as quickly and painlessly as possible for all involved (especially my kids). I went from trusting my ex- and promising to stand by him to confidently knowing that our marriage was over. Everyone works at their own pace and reaches decisions in the time frame which is right for them.

Many women heading down the path to divorce tell me that they plan to figure things out with their husband and just use one attorney so as to minimize fees and expenses. I've heard, "Well, my husband says that we can do this on our own and he said he's going to be fair, so I trust him." Did you trust him while you were married too? And what were the circumstances that brought you to this point? So, do you still trust him?

As much as you think you can, you absolutely will not be able to handle this by yourself. There are far too many things you have to consider and wording that has to be precise. Remember, the parenting plan and the financial settlement are legal documents that have a long shelf life. Most people don't have the forethought to anticipate every detail. Utilizing an expert, a divorce attorney, will help immensely. This is a must-have, not an optional item. You must hire an attorney to represent your best interests. Thinking you can do this by yourself is like thinking you can do your own open heart surgery. You would never do that, would you?

That being said, choosing an attorney can be tough. This is such a personal and emotional situation. You want someone who understands you and listens to you. You want someone who can negotiate on your behalf. You want someone who is savvy and smart. You want someone who is realistic, but is also looking out for your best interests. You want someone who is responsive and who treats you with respect (and not just as another divorce case). You want someone you can trust.

As with so many other professions, I turned to my network for recommendations for a good divorce attorney and selected a litigator about whom I had heard great things. I wanted someone who focused on divorce, not a general practitioner. Using my analogy, if I needed open heart surgery, I certainly wouldn't go to my general practitioner. I'm not saying you need to hire the most expensive attorney out there, but I will say that there are good divorce attorneys and bad divorce attorneys in terms of their knowledge of the law and their ability to communicate and negotiate.

I wanted to find a divorce attorney who was experienced and who had a good reputation in the eyes of other attorneys and judges. The last thing I wanted was to use an attorney who didn't get along with other attorneys or the judge and to have any sort of bias brought in with my case that would adversely affect me. You don't think this stuff can happen, but it does.

Another one of my requirements was to find an attorney who was going to be available in terms of timing. Divorce can be a long and lengthy process. Everything takes longer than it should. Add the emotional stress of divorce and the waiting and waiting for motions to be filed and judgments to be made, and you can literally feel like you are going crazy. Divorce is a lesson in patience … and a difficult lesson for some of us to tolerate. I needed an attorney who would return my calls or emails and generally feel the same sense of urgency that I had to keep the momentum moving forward.

I checked with my network and received several strong referrals. A few days later, I was sitting in an attorney's office. I explained my story. She listened patiently, handed me tissues when I needed to wipe my eyes, asked probing questions, and patiently explained the concept of divorce in Georgia. She suggested that I consider a process called Collaborative Law. She said that based on all she had heard from me, on how determined I was to not harm my children, and on how level-headed I was (constantly spouting my intent to "take the high road"), she thought I ought to at least consider "collaborative" as an option.

She affirmed what I knew in my heart: that litigating would be the worst possible thing for my kids. They would be dragged into court, dragged into the middle of this battle, and behavior would turn negative. They would witness what was going on. After meeting with me, she knew that protecting my kids was my top priority. She said that I might "get more" by going to court, but at the end of the day, that wouldn't be what was best for my kids. She was smart. She was good.

I told her I would give collaborative divorce a try. The fact is that if at any time during the collaborative process I found it wasn't working, I could immediately stop the process and return to formal divorce litigation. Fortunately, my ex- agreed to try the collaborative process as well. Here is a brief overview of what collaborative is all about (from the Collaborative Law Institute of Georgia).

Essentially, collaborative divorce involves a triage team of people who work together to bring resolution as quickly and fairly as possible. Both parties retain a lawyer trained in practicing collaborative. Both parties also work with a "coach" who helps the parents address their communication issues in order to assist them in creating a parenting plan. Lastly, both parties work with a single "financial neutral" who gathers information and works with them to craft a financial plan based on a realistic financial picture (by the way, I'm not sure why we use the word "party" because there is nothing festive about the divorce process – nothing!).

Ultimately, once all issues are resolved through meetings with the triage team, the attorneys draft a settlement agreement and the pleadings necessary to obtain a divorce. The pleadings are filed jointly. Basically, the judge is told that everything has been agreed to, and all he or she has to do is sign off on the paperwork. You typically don't even have to appear in court – ever.

The benefits of collaborative divorce are listed below. For the most part, I have to agree that my experience would support these benefits. In spite of requiring the triage team, our divorce did cost less than that of others I know who have used the traditional litigation format. We were very much involved with the entire team in the discussions and negotiations. Our divorce moved much more quickly than it would have if we had to rely on the traditional court calendars. From the day we started the collaborative process until the day our divorced was granted was approximately eight months.

~ **Lower Cost:** The collaborative process is generally less costly and time-consuming than litigation.

~ **Client Involvement:** The client is a vital part of the settlement team and has a greater sense of involvement in the decision making which affects their lives.

~ **Supportive Approach:** Each client is supported by their lawyer and coach in a manner that still allows the attorneys to work collaboratively with one another in resolving issues.

~ **Less Stress:** The process produces much less fear and anxiety than utilizing Court proceedings or the threat of such proceedings. Everyone can focus on settlement without the imminent threat of "going to Court."

~ **Win-Win Climate:** The collaborative process creates a positive climate that produces a more satisfactory outcome for both parties. The possibility actually exists for participants to create a climate that facilitates "win-win" settlements.

~ **Speed:** The speed of the collaborative process is governed by the parties rather than court calendars.

~ **Creativity:** The collaborative process encourages creative solutions in resolving issues.

~ **Clients in Charge:** The non-adversarial nature of the collaborative process shifts decision making into the hands of the clients where it belongs, rather than into the hands of a third party (the court).

Clearly, I have very strong opinions about what kind of divorce attorney you should seek. Whether you choose traditional litigation, mediation, or a collaborative process, what is important is finding a team of professionals who hold the same goals as you.

I have seen women hire lawyers who seem to believe that representing their clients fairly means they must engage in a legal battle on behalf of their clients. The constant bickering between attorneys is sometimes like watching children fight, both wanting to have the last word. I have seen numerous divorces prolonged due to attorneys creating more work for one another because of the back and forth filing of motions. In the end, it's more costly for you, and takes longer for the kids to start to feel closure (and the ability to get into a new routine).

You should find an attorney who believes that the end-goal is supporting options that highlight the best interests of your children, who encourages open communication, and who facilitates both parties being able to look forward and move on successfully in the future. It's a balance between finding someone who won't let you be run over, but who can also influence "the other side" to work effectively, fairly, efficiently and in the best interests of the children. It's about finding an attorney who believes in your same "high road" approach and does all he or she can to be on that journey with you, and who can influence your soon-to-be-ex- and his attorney to follow that path as well. It's about accepting responsibility and moving forward.

Divorce is one of the most stressful situations you will ever go through. Be prepared for that fact and accept it. The more you are able to remain focused and organized, the better off you will be, and the faster you will be able to get through this. Be realistic and honest! Think ahead. Consider your options. And then take it one day at a time! If you aren't a really organized person, ask a friend who is to help you out. The paperwork can be overwhelming and confusing, even for the most organized woman!

Your attorney will likely ask for you to start gathering these documents:

~ Tax returns for last 3 years

~ Pay stubs

~ Statements from all bank, savings, and investment accounts (cash, stocks, bonds, CD's, etc.)

~ Pension estimates

~ 401(k) and IRA statements

~ Profit sharing, bonus or stock option plans if eligible

~ Title to all property (real estate, vehicles)

~ Life insurance policies

If you aren't a planner by nature, you may need to really focus. Planning ahead alleviates a lot of last minute chaos. It will make everyone's life a little easier in the long-run. Here are some things you need to think about – some now, some later – but all things you will want to address at some point:

Things to think about ...

~ What are our assets? Liabilities? (your budget worksheet will help with this).

~ Will I be able to stay where I am living? Can I afford the mortgage and all expenses? If not, are there other affordable options nearby? How do we determine the amount of equity in our primary residence?

~ Where can I get a job? What skills are relevant to the job market?

~ Will I receive alimony? If so, how long can I rely on alimony to provide support?

~ What, if anything, will be considered a pre-marital asset?

~ What do I absolutely want from the house? Can I show documentation of anything considered to be a gift or inheritance to me? Do I have claims to any antiques, jewelry or other items of monetary or sentimental value?

~ Is the car titled to me?

~ How do I change my ex- as the beneficiary on my life insurance, retirement savings or other accounts?

~ Will I have to purchase health insurance? Who will cover the kids?

~ How do I determine the future value of pensions or stock options?

~ Who will take the children as the tax deduction on income tax returns?

~ What happens to the kids' college accounts? Are they still funded?

~ How do I change my will? How do I determine who to put down as guardians for my kids if something happens to me?

Divorce is a long and grueling process. It's not fun for anyone. It's emotional. It's tedious. It's frightening. You need to "own" the process and keep the momentum moving forward. Insist on regular meetings. Try to get your attorneys to feel the same speed for resolution. Navigate through your divorce as quickly as possible. Early on, someone told me that the longer the process rolls on, and the more time passes, the less "guilt" the other party will feel. Instead, a strong sense of entitlement will begin to build thus making it even harder to agree on a settlement. Don't settle in your settlement for the sake of speed, but settle fast! Does that make sense?

Ultimately, the collaborative process worked for us and our divorce was finalized. At the end of my story, I knew what I knew, and more importantly, I knew what I had to do for me and my kids. Finding forgiveness was huge. It didn't mean I wasn't going to hold my ex- accountable, it just meant that I was at peace. I won't go into all the detail about how our divorce proceedings progressed. Suffice to know, it's a painful process. My analogy was that I felt like I had climbed Mt. Everest, only to see another seemingly insurmountable peak ahead of me. At times it felt like it would never end. It wasn't an easy process, and still one I wouldn't wish on my worst enemy. It was full of emotional ups and downs with extreme highs and lows.

Bottom line: Consider collaborative. Explore it as an option. Find an attorney you trust. It will take longer than you want it to, and many days you will feel like you have just climbed Mt. Everest, only to see another mountain in front of you. Remember, this is an exercise in patience.

CELEBRATING 40:
WILL I EVER HAVE SEX AGAIN?

"A birthday is
just the first day of
another 365-day journey
around the sun.
Enjoy the trip."

~ Anonymous

I turned the big 4-0 in the midst of all this. The timing was so impeccable it's almost cliché. Here I was the divorcee, the single mom, turning 40. As usual, my friends were amazing. There is a whole group of us who always get together to celebrate birthdays. It's usually getting together for breakfast or lunch when the kids are at school. We typically stepped it up a notch when one of us was turning 40 and would go out to dinner or host a big party.

As my birthday approached, these awesome ladies rallied together and asked me how I would like to celebrate turning 40. I told them my vision was to spend the entire day with them just relaxing and talking while enjoying some time outside, followed by a great dinner somewhere. Honestly, I was thinking of a beautiful fall hike in the north Georgia mountains, but the idea of "hiking" didn't sit really well with some of the girls. Cindy suggested that we all fly to New York City and "hike" down 5th Avenue. Gena suggested we all go to the beach and "hike" on the sand. BINGO! With that great idea, the planning began, and a few weeks before my official birthday, me and ten of my closest friends drove to Florida to celebrate my 40th!

It was a perfect weekend. Perfect in every way, and I will never forget my friends for their love and support. We enjoyed the gorgeous weather and walked on the beach every day. We laughed. We talked. We ate great food. We gave each other facials. We built people pyramids and had wheel-barrow races on the beach (seriously!). We shopped. It was a perfect girls weekend, and frankly, an absolutely perfect way to ring in 40.

We were silly the entire time we were gone and took some great photos. We were goofing around on the drive down and at one point we stopped at the side of the road in rural Alabama near some haystacks. They "encouraged" me to climb on top of one of the haystacks for a "photo-op!"

Karen presented me with a photo album containing all the pictures from the trip. The photo of me on top of the hay stack was the cover photo. You know how normally you look at a photo of yourself and as women we typically critique our hair, our bodies, our make-up, our wrinkles … that's usually our first response, right? I surprised myself when Karen gave me the album. As I looked at the photo on the front of the album, the very first thing that popped into my mind was, "Oh my gosh, I look so HAPPY!" I surprised myself at how relaxed and stress free and just plain happy I looked! "HAPPY" is a very good thing and a very good place to be.

A few weeks later, Stacy and Ellen helped me to celebrate my 40th with a fun weekend at Kiawah Island. I decided I wanted to run the Kiawah Half Marathon to celebrate turning 40. It was amazing. What a powerful feeling of accomplishment (and another "HAPPY" photo) when we crossed that finish line. Guess all those hours on the elliptical really paid off and helped me build my endurance. We took advantage of running the half-marathon to talk and talk about all I had been through, and all that the future would bring. I think we entertained many a runner that day with our titillating conversation ... come to think of it, there did seem to be a number of people running at the same pace as us for a good part of the course. It's amazing how quickly 13.1 miles can pass when you are talking with your best friends.

Maybe it was turning 40, perhaps it was the divorce ... whatever it was, it was like the perfect storm and the perfect opportunity for me to get-away, try something new, laugh out loud, and feel a sense of pride and accomplishment. Don't forget to take care of you during this entire process. I think sometimes we get so busy making sure our kids are OK that we forget to take that extra time to focus on us.

I found I needed these moments of really good times, to help get me through those inevitable "bad" times. These were some of the really good times, but, as you can expect, there were plenty of sad and down-right pathetic moments during this whole process. It's amazing how your mind can keep you awake at night and how the thoughts tumble into your mind of things you will never experience again, or experience in the same way, and these thoughts keep getting bigger and bigger and keep crashing down on top of you over and over again. I remember nights just sitting in my bed crying and wondering how I was going to get through all of this ... just sobbing because life as I knew it was over for me and my children. It was devastating, and can be debilitating.

Here's an idea of how these thoughts, like waves in anticipation of a storm, just keep getting bigger and bigger ...

Thought one: my husband won't be here this weekend for all of us to go boating together ...

Thought two: actually my husband won't ever go boating with us again ...

Thought three: when summer is over, we won't be going to the "meet the teacher" night at school together ...

Thought four: in fact, this is my daughter's last year in elementary school and we won't be a happy family sitting at her graduation together ...

Thought five: forget elementary school graduation; we won't be at her high school graduation together ...

Thought six: in fact, we won't be taking photos together as she goes to her high school prom ...

Thought seven: speaking of photos, taking pictures at her wedding will be a nightmare because there won't be one big happy family moment ...

Thought eight: will she ever get married or will the effects of this divorce scar her forever and make her swear off relationships ...

Thought nine: if she does get married and gets pregnant, who will be with her when she delivers the baby? (both of my parents were at the hospital when I delivered her and it was so wonderful having them both waiting with me) ...

Thought ten: who will my grandchild spend his or her first Christmas with? ...

Phew! See how these crashing waves of thoughts work? They just get bigger and bigger and seem insurmountable.

Another one of the overwhelming thoughts that entered my mind was "I'll never have sex again." Don't laugh. It's true. Wouldn't this thought cross your mind too? At 40 years old, I had the body of a middle-aged woman who had delivered two kids. I felt good in jeans and a sweater, but naked? That's another story! I had a pretty flat stomach when I stood up, but as soon as I sat down – poof – the baby pooch appeared. And, my thighs and butt looked like they had been hit with a hail storm. (Can someone tell me why exactly God created cellulite?) The thought of letting anyone new see all of this was frightening. I knew, just knew, I would never have sex again.

Then God put a new friend in my life. I met her one evening through a mutual friend and immediately connected with Allison. I liked her "tell it like it is" attitude. I volunteered to pick her up and drive her to a meeting we were both going to two days later. I was still pretty fragile at this point. I hadn't reached my forgiveness moment yet and was still really bitter and really scared about what my life had in store for me. She didn't know my whole story or the timing of it all. Allison simply knew I was going through a divorce.

She hopped into my car with her great big smile and her wonderful personality and asked how I was doing. I gave some pat answer that I was "fine." Her response still cracks me up to this day because I needed to hear it, but had no idea that I did. She reached out and put her hand on my leg, and said, "Don't worry! You will have sex again." I burst out laughing! I had only met Allison one other time, literally for like five minutes, and for her to just come out and say this (did I mention we were on our way to a meeting at church?) was hilarious. I told her, "No, I won't. No man is going to see my jiggly butt."

She laughed as well, and assured me I was wrong ... then went on to tell me that she was almost an expert on the subject. I may not have mentioned that Allison's first husband was unfaithful to her, they divorced when she had two young kids, she had remarried a few years earlier, and was now seven months pregnant – thus proving you will have sex again!

Bottom line: Take care of you! Make time for you. Laugh with your girlfriends. And, you will have sex again!

Being There for Your Friends: It's A Two-Way Street

"A friend is one
of the nicest things
you can have,
and one of the best
things you can be."

~ Douglas Pagels

I've talked quite a bit about how wonderful my friends were, but I also need to warn you that your friends may change a little bit too. Some may become a bit distant. Some may "protest" too much about how healthy their own marriages are, and claim that this would never happen to them. Cut them some slack, and don't be offended.

If only I had a dollar for every person who said, "Never in a million years did I think this would happen to you." Admit it. You and your husband, or you and your friends have had conversations as you are driving home from a dinner party as to whom in the group seemed to be rocky and would be most likely to get divorced. Am I right? That's something that comes up in conversations most often when driving home from an event with lots of couples present. To my knowledge, my ex- and I never made it on that list. We appeared to have it all together. Values. Love. Respect. A beautiful family. By society's standards, one might say that we had it all.

Divorce, when it happens to others (especially those in your social circle) really makes you think. As word got out that we were getting divorced, I could almost feel people assessing their own marriages. Friends started turning the mirror to their own relationships. I had friends admit to me that my divorce scared them to death because they started to really think about their own relationships and how much love was present. They told me they started wondering whether perhaps their husbands were capable of cheating on them. I don't blame some of my friends for being paranoid. If it can happen to me, it can happen to any one of us. That certainly creates some pressure and some stress.

On the other end of the spectrum, friends who had in prior times confided in me about their frustrations with their husband suddenly started over-emphasizing how happy they were. I think "you doth protesteth too much." I had friends boldly and bluntly say things like, "Well, I know for a fact that my husband would never do that to me." Yeah, well, I thought my husband never would either.

You can't get angry or frustrated with comments like this. You have to be there for them as they deal with their own insecurities and doubts about how quickly life can change. I would like to think that our situation helped more than a few couples to slow down a bit, to communicate more, to reaffirm their love ... it's a reality check. The ripple effect of our divorce extended beyond my ex-, me and our kids. It hit our friends like a ton of bricks too.

Our friends were shocked and hurt. Our divorce impacted them as well. Gone were the days of all of us, as couples and as families, getting together for dinner, or to play games, or to even go on vacation. Suddenly our friends were forced to explain the concept of divorce to their kids, and frankly, many of them weren't ready to broach that subject yet given the ages of their children. It raised a lot of questions and created a lot of tough dialogue. Be patient with them.

Being a divorced woman creates its own little bond and its own little clique. It's kind of like when a parent dies. Friends who have experienced the death of parent seem to "get it" just a little better than others. Obviously, it's the same with women who have gone through a divorce and especially women who have gotten divorced due to extramarital affairs. It creates a bond and a kinship ... a kind of "while my story may be a little different, I totally get what you are going through" kind of relationship that can overshadow all other differences.

What do you say when you hear that someone is getting divorced? I think our first inclination is to say, "I'm sorry." I know this is what I had said to people in the past, and this is what people said to me. I got tired of it. I appreciated their empathy, but I didn't want their sympathy. I was sorry that my fantasy of "happily ever after" wasn't happening and I was sorry that my children had to go through the trials of being from a divorced family.

I started correcting people. I would say, "Please don't be sorry for me, but please be sorry for the situation." I have spoken with many women since that time who are going through a divorce and I think nearly every one of them has been bothered by the "I'm sorry" comments. People mean well ... my advice is to be careful of how things are worded. It is so much more meaningful to share, "I'm sorry that you are going through this situation and if there is anything I can do to help, please let me know."

Getting divorced fuels gossip and talk and the news of another marriage on the rocks and heading to splitsville spreads like wildfire. I found it so uncomfortable knowing that me, and my marriage, were the subject of so many conversations. Feeling like people felt "sorry" for me was like adding salt to a wound (and, as I have since heard, for many others as well!).

In the beginning going to church each Sunday alone with the kids was heartbreaking. I would vow to be strong, but week after week I would end up crying while sitting in the pews listening to the music or the sermon. I had friends suggest that perhaps I should take a break from church so that I wouldn't be crying in front of everyone. Are you serious? If I can't cry at church, then where can I cry? There is no shame in going to a place of worship to be sad and to try and figure out God's plan for my new life.

My shame came in learning to let go of the dream, and realizing just how deep in the sand I had buried my head in pursuit of that dream. Remember, I was NEVER going to be one of those divorced women … it would never happen to me. There is no shame in at least believing in the dream.

I do still occasionally feel embarrassed by the stigma of being divorced. It's as if I feel that I wasn't successful in keeping my marriage alive. I feel like a failure. Simple things like introducing me and my kids to someone and having to use a different last name, or having to change my name on every account and legal document out there (all the utilities, the newspaper, the gym membership, and the list goes on) was a reminder that my marriage had failed.

Be prepared for the fall-out to continue for months and even years after your divorce is finalized, and be prepared with your responses when people don't know you have divorced. For a good year after we were supposed to have moved to Denver, I still had people coming up to me saying, "I thought you moved to Denver," or, "Good to see you back visiting us here in Atlanta." I never wanted to make someone else feel badly, so I always tempered my response with a gentle comment that I had divorced and the kids and I were pleased to still be here in gorgeous Atlanta. Those could be some awkward moments for some people, and I never wanted them to feel badly.

To this day, I hate this. I hate feeling like a statistic. I sometimes feel like I invested 19 years of my life, only to have it end, dashing my fairytale forever-after with it. I hate to think that my kids don't know the security of a loving, stable family unit complete with a biological mom and dad still living under the same roof. Yet, I know deep in my heart, that I can't let these negative thoughts overpower me.

The additional observation I will make with respect to your circle of friends is that some people may start to act just a bit differently with you around as a single woman, instead of as part of a married couple. Suddenly, you could be considered a threat, as opposed to just one of the gang. This can sometimes create an awkward tension. We are all a pretty huggy and touchy group of friends – both men and women. We all hug hello and goodbye when we see each other. It was always very natural. But, as my divorce became final and I was officially a single woman, I started to sense a bit of caution on the part of some friends if I hugged their husbands.

My behavior hadn't changed, but certainly my circumstances and my status had. I vividly recall intentionally changing my behavior and pulling back a little bit. I was certainly more cognizant of how other people might perceive my behavior and I adjusted my guardrails accordingly. There was no such thing as "harmless flirting." Again, this is something to be aware of. You don't want to create unnecessary concerns or problems or create an issue out of nothing.

Be patient with your friends as they adjust to your divorce. It seems backwards to say that, right? Shouldn't it be your friends demonstrating patience to you? Yes, AND, that patience needs to be reciprocated. The best intentions sometimes come across differently. Don't react ... or over-react.

Bottom line: Be aware of what your friends are going through too. Consider their perspective and the impact all of this has had on them. Don't focus on the negative. You aren't a statistic!

Taking Pride in New Accomplishments: I Conquered the Grill!

"The difficulties
of life are intended to
make us better, not bitter."

~ Dan Reeves

I've always been pretty self-sufficient. That being said, there were a few things that I never felt comfortable doing, and certain things became my ex-'s responsibility. I wanted to continue to do these things, but I didn't have him here to do them. It's funny, but two things really stand out on that list, and I remember feeling like I had won the Super Bowl, Wimbledon, and the World Series when I first attempted, and mastered, these two things on my own.

Don't judge my two items! These may be things you already do well. Just recognize that we all have those things which we just don't do – but want to still have done. For me, it was starting the grill and cooking out, and driving the boat (particularly settling it back onto the boat lift).

I was determined to learn to use my grill, but it intimidated me beyond belief. Why in the world would I want to light a match next to a great big flammable container of propane? I knew I had to get over this fear. I called Kathleen. She's got a huge grill and cooks out all the time. "Kath," I said, "I've got this gorgeous outdoor grill with lots of different levels and burners and knobs and dials ... and I'm intimidated beyond belief." Kathleen was thrilled to come over and show me how easy it was to get it started. Easy? Yes! Liberating? You have no idea! Suddenly I was grilling all the time. My kids loved it. I loved it. Watch out world, here comes Monique, master griller.

As you can imagine, the boat was an even bigger hurdle for me. This was a huge vehicle that cost a lot of money and could harm people if I messed up while driving or docking it. You have to get over the fear and the paralysis, and I did just that. I clearly remember the first time I took the boat out on my own. I took a calming breath, said a little prayer, and patiently tried to remember all the different steps. You know what? The boat started and we were backing out of the dock before I knew it.

Driving is easy ... it's pulling back onto the boat lift that kept my adrenalin flowing. It finally came time to come back in. Thankfully, my prayers were answered and it wasn't a windy day with a strong current. I pulled back into the boat lift so smoothly, so calmly, so confidently (on the outside!) that you would think I had been docking boats for a lifetime. I felt absolutely incredible!

Thank goodness for small (and large) victories. Thank goodness for those feelings of accomplishment. When going through a divorce, you need to bottle up all those great feelings when you have them because goodness knows there will be plenty of times when you need to draw on them.

You will have days, even weeks, where you feel like you have succeeded in getting through your divorce. Everything is going well. You are crying less and laughing more, and suddenly, something will happen that will set you back. You will feel as if you have fallen right back to the bottom of the canyon and have to start to climb back out again. Store up the feelings from those good times. You will need to draw on them at other times.

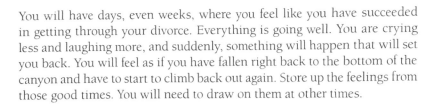

3 Goals for the Next Year

What 3 goals do I want to accomplish in the next 12 months? Write them down. Be specific. Work towards achieving them. I promise when you look back at this list in 12 months and you have completed everything you wrote down you will feel a tremendous sense of accomplishment!

1.

2.

3.

Bottom line: Figure out what is on your list of things you want to master and do them! You can! And, you'll love the feeling of accomplishment!

SPENDING TIME ALONE:
LEARN TO RELISH AND RECHARGE

*"You can always choose
to perceive things differently.
You can focus on what's
wrong in your life, or you can
focus on what's right."*

~ Marianne Williamson

The first time my ex- had the kids alone for the weekend was traumatic and tumultuous for me. It seems silly now, but I was so concerned that they wouldn't have anything to eat at his apartment (I had always done the grocery shopping) that I sent food with them. I wanted to be sure they didn't starve. In retrospect, this is kind of funny, but at the time, it was my way of continuing to take care of them.

I held it together as I got the kids ready to go. I kissed them goodbye and told them to have fun, then I shut the door and burst into tears. How many times had I dreamed of having a "free" weekend with nothing to do, no one to take care of, no one to bother me. In these daydreams, I had visions of reading books while wrapped up in a blanket on the back porch, sleeping in, going to the gym without any time crunch, going for long walks, manicures, pedicures, dinners with friends, and the list would go on.

The reality is that once my kids were gone, I was really at a loss for what to do. I struggled that weekend. I couldn't focus. I wasn't sure what I wanted to do. By the time the kids came home on Sunday afternoon, I'm not sure I had accomplished much of anything, and I certainly didn't feel rested and relaxed.

As moms, most of us are used to constantly "doing" for our kids: we're fixing meals, washing clothes, helping with homework, running them to extracurricular activities, getting them ready for bed, packing lunches, and the list goes on and on.

Studies have shown it's NOT the divorce itself that negatively affects children, but rather the parents fighting that takes place before, during and after the divorce. It's the parents' inability to successfully co-parent and "share" the children. I knew I needed to make sure that when my kids spent time with their dad, that it was "guilt-free." Every time they left, I smiled and told them to have a great time, but inside I was crying.

Ultimately I came to realize that I needed to learn to accept, and perhaps even to cherish, those times alone. I could either be miserable, or I could learn to embrace these moments. The choice was up to me, and I alone held the power to make that decision.

One friend called me in tears one Saturday morning. Her ex- had taken the kids on vacation for a week. This was only day two, and she wasn't sure of what to do with herself. I asked her what she used to love to do on the weekends before her kids were born. "I would go hiking all day long," she replied. "Then go hiking all day long," I said. She hadn't even considered that as a possibility.

Being a single mom is tough. It's tiring. It can sometimes feel thankless. Learn to relish those times when you do have some free time for yourself. It's hard to do in the beginning. We aren't sure what to do with ourselves. Figure out what makes you happy, or what at least takes your mind off the fact that your kids aren't with you, and do more of that. It will get easier with time, I promise.

If I had a free weekend, defined as no responsibility for anyone but me, what 10 things would I do?

1.

2.

3.

4.

5.

6.

7.

8.

9.

10.

Bottom line: Learn to accept, and relish, your time alone. Take the time to discover (or re-discover) who you are and what you like to do.

Saying Thank You:
You're at 100%

"Big changes in our lives are more or less a second chance."

- Harrison Ford

Back when the F-word was really the F-word, and not forgiveness. Back when I was still dropping the F-bomb, my ex- had the audacity to tell me that I would one day thank him for this. "F*** YOU," I replied, "I will never thank you for ruining our family."

In the early days of our marriage when I would tell my ex- he was right about something, he would come back with a funny retort like, "Yup, I'm running a 99.982% average on being right this month." It was always kind of cute and funny. He loved hearing that he was right.

Guess what? He was 100% right on this one. You were RIGHT! YOU WERE RIGHT!! I do want to thank him for this. He didn't ruin our family. I am at a stage now where I can look back and see that he saved me from a life of feeling unappreciated. He saved me from a life where our kids didn't regularly witness true love, true respect, true communication and true partnership. I look back on that marriage and I am so thankful that I am no longer in it. I'm sorry that I went through that experience. I'm sorry that my kids went through that experience. I wouldn't wish that level of physical pain or emotional hurt on my worst enemy. But, in retrospect, it's the best thing that ever happened to us.

This is so hard to admit, but I lived in a fairy tale. I knew I wasn't loved the way I wanted to be, deserved to be, ought to be. There was a lack of respect and a lack of love. I made excuses and rationalized it as "that's just the way he is" but I knew deep inside I needed better, deserved more, and wasn't truly happy. I let myself feel this way.

Yes, looking back on all this, I do feel so incredibly stupid and naive. Putting pen to paper and seeing all these scenarios play out it all seems so obvious where my ex- was headed, but at the time, I wasn't connecting the dots on any of these things.

Clearly, I love motivational quotes. I found this one hanging in my cousin's bathroom in Michigan. She hung it there so her kids would read it when they were sitting on the toilet. I thought that was pretty smart. What a captive audience! I read this and thought it pretty much summed it all up for me. It's called the Desiderata. I would like to give due credit to the author, but from what I can tell, there are a few different opinions out there on who wrote it. To the best of my knowledge, it was written by a gentleman named Max Ehmann in the 1920's. I think Max must have been a pretty wise man!

Desiderata

Go placidly amid the noise and the haste, and remember what peace there may be in silence.

As far as possible, without surrender, be on good terms with all persons.

Speak your truth quietly and clearly and listen to others,

even to the dull and the ignorant; they too have their story.

Avoid loud and aggressive persons; they are vexatious to the spirit.

If you compare yourself with others, you may become vain or bitter, for always there will be greater and lesser persons than yourself.

Enjoy your achievements as well as your plans. Keep interested in your own career, however humble; it is a real possession in the changing fortunes of time.

Exercise caution in your business affairs, for the world is full of trickery.

But let this not blind you to what virtue there is; many persons strive for high ideals,

and everywhere life is full of heroism. Be yourself. Especially do not feign affection.

Neither be cynical about love, for in the face of all aridity and disenchantment,

it is as perennial as the grass.

Take kindly the counsel of the years, gracefully surrendering the things of youth.

Nurture strength of spirit to shield you in sudden misfortune.

But do not distress yourself with dark imaginings. Many fears are born of fatigue and loneliness.

Beyond a wholesome discipline, be gentle with yourself.

You are a child of the universe, no less than the trees and the stars; you have a right to be here.

And whether or not it is clear to you, no doubt the universe is unfolding as it should.

Therefore be at peace with God, whatever you conceive Him to be.

And whatever your labors and aspirations, in the noisy confusion of life, keep peace in your soul.

With all its sham, drudgery, and broken dreams, it is still a beautiful world.

Be cheerful. Strive to be happy.

Bottom line: Be open to being right, or wrong. Marriage is hard work. You have to put effort into it every single day. Read the Desiderata once a year … it's full of really good advice.

BECOMING FRIENDS:
WE'LL BE LIKE BRUCE AND DEMI

"Treat others as you want them to treat you because what goes around comes around."

~ Anonymous

As all of this "unfolded" and my ex- and I were debating the details of our parenting plan (the new name for "custody agreements") and our financial settlement (the new name for determining who gets what from a financial perspective), he repeatedly would talk about how he saw us being "like Bruce and Demi" in the future. I would laugh, snort or roll my eyes every time he said this. He, of course, was referring to the tabloid-worthy story of how Bruce and Demi have stayed great friends since their divorce even going so far as to vacation together (even after Demi married Ashton Kutcher). It became clear to me that as he had considered our divorce, he had romanticized this notion that we would become the "Bruce and Demi" of our area.

It was funny to me how often he referred to them ... always on a first name basis like they were best friends and had lots of conversations about how to manage so well post-divorce. In fact, I too admired what I had read in *People Magazine* about how well the former Mr. and Mrs. Willis (I don't know them well enough to have a first name relationship with them!) handled their relationship post-divorce. It did seem to be the best thing to do for the sake of the children. Goodness knows there are enough examples of Hollywood relationships gone bad where the innocent children witness horrific behaviors and accusations on the part of each parent about the other.

I realized I had two choices. We could act like Kathleen Turner and Michael Douglas in the movie *War of the Roses* where they destroy the house fighting over items in their divorce (literally fighting over the proverbial "toaster"), or we could put on our big girl panties and deal with the hand we've been dealt.

Bruce and Demi we will never be, but we are capable of having productive conversations with one another, especially about our children. And as tough as these conversations once were, they have gotten easier with time. Every moment of pain I endured throughout this ordeal becomes irrelevant when I hear my kids make comments about how great it is that their mom and dad still get along.

I doubt my ex- and I will ever be like Bruce, Demi and Ashton and all vacation together with our kids, (and I have also learned to "never say never"). However, we absolutely must communicate with one another in order to raise our kids properly. We have to talk about our expectations, about grades, about discipline, about extra-curricular activities – essentially about everything our kids have going on in their lives. My kids want both mom and dad to be at their sporting events or school activities. It's the kids who are hurt the most if their dad doesn't show up for something at school. It behooves me to keep him informed, and vice versa. In retrospect, there are great lessons to be learned from watching how Bruce and Demi have handled their situation.

Learning to communicate and trust one another wasn't easy to do. I can't make this sound like suddenly the divorce was over and we were able to have wonderful conversations with each other. We had to learn to begin talking again in small increments. For a long time it was easier to simply communicate via email about who had to be where and when. That's a perfectly OK way to start the dialogue … at least it's dialogue! It's easy to communicate that way, and it's easy to keep the emotion out. As we progressed, we started finding it easier to talk on the phone to share updates with respect to the kids. We've even started meeting for a quarterly cup of coffee (at Starbucks®, of course!).

I know my children want to see me communicating with their new step-mom just as much as I'm communicating with their dad. They see it, and feel it, when there are awkward silences between us when we are all at a sporting event together.

When my ex- first announced that he and his girlfriend were going to get married, I called his fiancé and suggested that we get together. My friends thought I was crazy. They thought I was seriously deranged and wondered what in the world I would have to speak with her about. I answered that question very easily. I wanted to know that she was a mom at heart; that she had that "mom instinct" that would be on whenever she was with my kids. I wanted to know if they were in a busy parking lot and a car started to back out that her first instinct would be to grab my children's hands.

That coffee was life-changing. I like his wife (at least I can say my ex-has good taste in women!). We spoke for several hours. Under different circumstances, we might have been good friends. The reality is that we are able to have conversations mom-to-mom about our kids and our dreams and goals for them. Her youngest son and my two kids are all one year apart from each other in age and they get along great. Her son spends a lot of time at my house. The first time he came over, my kids commented that it was "odd" that he was there since he was their dad's new wife's son. They realized this was not typical behavior, and I knew they appreciated it. It's not a big deal anymore at all; it's just a way of life. The children are all innocent parties to this entire situation. They are truly casualties. They don't need to be punished.

We have even gotten to the point where we can joke about some things together. When they married, her initials became my old initials so I gave her a great monogrammed straw bag someone had given to me that I had stuck in the back of my closet. I told her that she might as well put it to good use. My kids thought that was pretty cool! That gesture went a long way.

At the end of the day, I still think children belong with their mothers, but at least when they are over there, I know who they are with, and, I know it's not some person whom I hate, whom my kids hate, or whom hates me, or my kids. I can't imagine how rough it would be if my kids hated going over there because their dad's wife was mean to them. We don't have any of that drama to deal with for which I am very grateful.

Whatever method we use to communicate, I know that it is in the best interest of our children to know that we are indeed communicating with each other. I know it's important. They have commented on it. They have recognized how monumental it is (and perhaps how unique based on the experiences that some of their friends have shared) that their dad and I are able to talk to each other again.

I strongly encourage you to get along for the sake of your kids. Getting along doesn't have to mean being best friends and hugging every time you see one another. It does mean speaking respectfully to one another and never, ever degrading the other parent in front of the children. I can't emphasize this point enough. It seems obvious, but I've seen countless parents violate this code of conduct and the people they hurt the most are the innocent souls of their children who watch their parents' love for each other turn to hate. I see the joy on my kids' faces when they see us all talking or laughing together and it reaffirms for me over and over again just how important it is to take the high road.

Bottom line: Bruce and Demi really are onto something! Consider the importance to your kids of seeing both of their parents participate in raising them together! Recognize that their future will be defined by actions and decisions you make starting now.

MOVING FORWARD:
IMAGINE THE POSSIBILITIES

"Let go and let God."

~ Anonymous

I could see the future and I knew in my heart that everything was going to be OK ... better than OK. I knew we had all survived, and now it was time for all of us to thrive ... me, my ex-, the kids! We all settled into a comfortable routine.

I said this wasn't going to be a faith-based book, and I also said that my faith is very important to me. I talk with God ... a lot. Always have, always will. I'm not gifted at "prayer," but I do feel like I can carry on a good conversation with almost anyone, and that is how I talk with God. It's just a conversation between me and Him.

Believe me. There were lots of conversations with God. In the beginning, my prayers were that my ex- and I would reconcile. When I realized that wasn't possible, most of my conversations with God had me crying and wondering what would become of my life and that of my kids. I never asked, "why me, God." Why not me? Why should I be different from all the other women in the world going through a divorce. My conversations started to shift focus to asking God to give me faith, patience and strength to get through all the days in front of me.

I felt the need to have some sort of tangible object that I could wear to remind me that God was with me. I asked a friend to design a necklace for me that would reach past my heart and that I could hold on to tightly when I needed to. The resulting necklace that my friend designed was exactly what I needed. It reached past my heart in length, and was strong and sturdy for me to grab a hold of when I prayed. I had three silver bars hung on it each stamped with one word. I used the words that I was asking God for help with – namely, patience, strength and faith. I added a small round disc to the necklace that said, "Philippians 4:13," which reads, "I can do all things through Him who gives me strength," because I knew I would never be able to get through this without God. Finally, I added a gemstone, a peridot, which is the birthstone for both of my children because I wanted a tangible symbol that every decision I made and every action I took had to be in their best interests. I wore that necklace every single day for months. My friends teased me that I was going to erode the words off it because I would hold on to that necklace so much. It's funny, but it brought me great comfort.

I am not familiar with the book of Jeremiah in the Bible. Very shortly after word of "The Pronouncement" came out, my wonderful and caring friends began to send me cards of support. My friend Kim sent me a card in which she had written a scripture verse. I loved the verse and what it said. I had never heard it before. That same week I received a card from my friend Deb in which she had written the same verse. The verse? Jeremiah 29:11. It quickly became my favorite and it's become my staple verse for my life. Jeremiah 29:11 says, "For I know the plans I have for you, declares the Lord, plans to prosper you and not to harm you, plans to give you hope and a future." That gave me hope, and I knew in my heart that God did and does have a plan for me and that I needed to trust in God that His plan would be "perfect for me."

A few months later, I couldn't sleep one night and I found myself grabbing a magazine off my nightstand. As I read the magazine, I turned the page to an article about a 39 year-old divorced woman with two kids who was lamenting to her friends about how she was tired of dating and not finding the "perfect" man for her. Her friends suggested that she ask God for help. How ironic, I thought. This woman is like me: same age, two kids, divorced. The message in the article was that her friends told her that God wants us to pray very specifically for what we want ... "by prayer and petition." They urged their friend to literally write a list of what she was looking for in a future husband. She did, and she presented this list to God as part of her prayers. She prayed very specifically for what type of man she was seeking. God delivered! They met, they married and they lived happily ever after! It was a fairy-tale ending. And, I love happy endings.

I vividly recall lying in bed with a feeling of contentment after reading that story. How nice to see that it can work out for a 39-year-old divorced mom of two. I literally began laughing out loud. People watching me would have thought I was nuts. The thought of getting into another relationship, let alone dating, hadn't even entered my mind. I was still very raw emotionally, and I certainly wasn't going to introduce my kids to anyone. But, as I lay there, it humored me to think about what traits I would put on my "list." I know it sounds nuts, but at the time it added some humor and hope to a desperate time in my life!

Here's what I put on my list...

My list:

Christian – faith level on par with mine

Charitable – loves to give back and help others

Loves his family – very involved with them and always there for them

Outgoing and social – loves to meet and talk with people

"Corporate-y" – knows the world of business and how to operate in it

Considerate and kind – always treats other respectfully

Not afraid of the kitchen – capable of cooking a real meal

Great communicator – freely able to express what is on his mind

Emotionally wide open – enough said!

Planner – organized and on top of things

Charming and funny – great sense of humor with the ability to make me laugh

Loves kids – specifically someone who would enjoy my children and love them as much as any biological parent ... and someone whom my kids would love right back

Physically fit and attractive – someone who would enjoy going walking or bike riding with me, someone whom I would be drawn to physically

Adventurous – up for trying new things and exploring new places

Challenging, yet content – always ready to take on bigger and better things, but not at the risk of losing contentment with the little things in life

Divorced – someone who knew the challenges of marriage, and how much work it takes, and preferably someone who didn't already have children since it can add so much complexity to an already challenging situation

I finished my list and laughed out loud again! In my mind, this described my "perfect" man, but I also thought, "You could probably ask one hundred women to put together a list, and it might look exactly like this." I decided to add two more items to my list. I literally said out loud, "OK God, you said to be specific, 'by prayer and petition.' I would also like him to be tall … I'd say 6' tall would be perfect, so he can wrap his arms around me and give me a great big covering hug, and I'd like him to be able to sing … not just anything, but specifically country music."

At that, I finished my list. There! How's that for specific. I laughed again thinking about the last two points I added.

Seriously? A height requirement? I really wanted someone whom I could look up to literally and figuratively. Being 5'2" tall, I really wanted someone whose arm would fit perfectly right over my shoulders when we were standing next to each other, and someone whom I would have to reach up to kiss while standing on my tiptoes.

Country music? Not sure where that thought had come from as I wasn't a huge country music fan, but I had always loved listening to the clear voice of a country crooner sharing his story.

I turned out the light to go to sleep, and decided to add a P.S. I said, "God, I'm so not ready for this yet, but when the timing is right, it would be great if you would present this person to me on a silver platter. The idea of dating many men is unappealing to me. I sure would appreciate it if you would just make this one appear." I signed off with, "Thanks God, I really appreciate it. Good night."

I'm not kidding. That's how it all happened. By the time I woke up the next morning, the night before was a distant memory and life as a single mom, going through a divorce, working, taking care of two kids, had resumed.

After the months of having negative thoughts reeling through my mind, it was fun to think positively and daydream about the future! I tell this to women today who have the play-by-play of negativity and revenge running through their minds. I hear from women who go running every day and are all-consumed rehashing the past or fantasizing about revenge. I remember all too clearly those days. I suggest that they change the film-reel to something more positive … to some I even suggest making "the list."

Just for kicks, take a few minutes to make YOUR list. What traits are important to you? Be specific! More importantly, have fun!

My list:

1.

2.

3.

4.

5.

6.

7.

8.

9.

10.

(Now, isn't this more fun than thinking negative thoughts?)

Bottom line: PACE: Positive Attitude Changes Everything. Think positive thoughts about the future. Trust me, it's a lot more fun than having negative thoughts consume you every day! And, you never know!

ENJOYING GOD'S SENSE OF HUMOR:
A DATE, SERIOUSLY?

*"God has a plan
and it's perfect for me."*

~ from the song "God's Plan"
written by Justin Honaman

Several months later I was invited to introduce some high school students who were being presented with an award for their incredible leadership in the community. I thanked them for the invitation, but replied that I wouldn't be able to make it. It was a school night, I couldn't leave the kids home alone, and I didn't want to pay for a kid-sitter. The night before this event, my ex- called to say he was coming to town and asked if he could have the kids that next evening. I said yes, and then in a move that still doesn't make sense to me, I called the person who had invited me to the event and said I would be there. Now, why I didn't spend my first free night in months going over to a friend's house to talk, or going on a long walk, or reading a book, getting a manicure, going out to dinner, going to the gym, going shopping or doing anything else on my list of "here's what I would do if I suddenly had a free night for just me," is beyond me. But no, instead, I chose to put on a suit and drive to downtown Atlanta.

To make matters even more strange, after I called and told them I would be there, I realized I didn't have enough gasoline in my car to get downtown and back again, and this was during the gas shortage. I hadn't seen a gas station in days in our area that had gas. I went out at lunch to see if I could find a station with gas, and came across a fuel truck unloading at the local station. I got in line with about 40 other cars and waited, and finally filled my tank. Why I chose to then "waste" this precious, and expensive, gas to drive downtown is still beyond me, but at the time, I didn't blink an eye.

I arrived at the event just a few minutes early, walked in, paused, and looked around to get "the lay of the land." As I gazed to the right side of the room, I noticed a guy walking towards me. He confidently held out his hand and introduced himself, "Hi, I'm Justin Honaman." I shook his hand, introduced myself and we naturally and easily began talking about anything and everything. Turns out he was there to present an award as well, and as the evening progressed we stuck together with our conversation never hitting a dull note.

We had a great time talking with each other and really connected, but as far as I was concerned, it wasn't going to go any further than that. I didn't even consider the possibility of anything moving forward between us. While I was legally separated (which meant I could legally date others), I was not yet divorced, and I was a mother to two children. He was single (divorced, no kids) and, as I discovered, five years younger than me. We had a great time talking and hanging out, exchanged the requisite business cards, and said our goodbyes at the end of the evening. That was that.

What that evening did provide me with was hope. As I explained to Kathleen the next day, I was surprised at how easily and openly we communicated. I felt like I had known him forever. It gave me hope for my future that when the timing was right, I would be able to meet someone with whom I would be able to feel such an instant connection.

Fast forward one month. Life had continued to move forward. I was healing and feeling really good. I told my friends that emotionally, mentally and physically, I felt the strongest I had ever felt in my entire life. I had forgiven, and I'd been a better person every day since then. Life was good. I felt great.

It was a Friday afternoon and I was driving to a meeting. Suddenly all traffic stopped on the express-way because a tractor-trailer overturned blocking all south-bound lanes. Ordinarily, I would have turned around and called it a day. By the time I took the back roads to get to this meeting, it was going to be half-over anyway. For some reason, I stuck to it. I arrived, an hour late, breathlessly raced in and grabbed the last remaining seat. I sat down, took a deep breath to calm down, and looked up ... and guess who was sitting directly across the room from me? Justin Honaman. He smiled and waved. I smiled back. It was great to see him again. I hadn't seen or talked with him since the night we met a month earlier, but again I felt an instant connection. He got up to get a Diet Coke® from the back of the room, walked by, squeezed my shoulder and said hello.

After the meeting, it was clear that he was loitering nearby waiting to talk with me as I wrapped up a conversation with someone else. He pretty much cut to the chase and asked what I thought about going out on a date with a younger guy who didn't have any kids. I responded with some quirky comment about that depended on what he thought about going out with an older woman who had two amazing children. We agreed to meet for a drink the next night.

We did meet the next night for one glass of wine, followed by several cups of tea. The conversation kept flowing and flowing and flowing, and we weren't ready to call it quits (hence the move to the coffee shop for tea!). I have never connected with anyone the way I did with Justin that night, or in the months to come. During the course of the evening, Justin shared with me that he liked to sing. In fact, he sang every Sunday as a worship leader with the kids at Buckhead Church. He continued and told me that had released an album three years earlier. "What kind of album," I asked. "Country music!" WOW! I started to laugh a little thinking about "the list."

Out of the blue, I asked Justin how tall he was. I think he thought that was an odd question. "Six feet," he replied. "Six feet exactly," I pestered, "or five feet eleven inches, or six feet one inch?" "No," he said, "a straight six feet." WOW! I laughed a bit more, but didn't take it any further than that.

How's that for serendipitous? God does indeed answer prayers, and certainly has His own opinion on when the timing is "right."

I talked with my mom and told her that I had met someone and that God's timing was pretty unexpected, and yet exciting. As usual, she encouraged me to follow my heart. She said she trusted that I knew what I was doing and told me she couldn't wait to meet Justin.

I met Justin's family and after that first meeting I told my mom I felt like I had known them forever. I felt like I had been curled up on their couch having a great conversation with them for years, not like this was the first time we had met.

I talked with my Pastor, and fully expected him to tell me that I was rushing things, that I was rebounding, and that I needed to slow down. Instead, he commented on how level-headed and aware I was being, and encouraged me. He met Justin and immediately commented on our chemistry and gave us his blessing which meant so much.

I started to tell my girlfriends and I got a mixture of pure excitement, cautious enthusiasm, and loving concern. Essentially, all the normal reactions I would have expected! Most of my friends were supportive and couldn't wait to meet this man whom I couldn't stop smiling about. Several friends did question the relationship and assumed it was a "rebound." My response was always the same: "If this was you, I love you enough as a friend to ask you the exact same thing. I would be worried about you; worried that you were rushing into things and not seeing clearly. But, I assure you, I have thought about this long and hard. There is something real to this. This is different." Most of my friends responded to that. My mantra became, "don't steal my joy." And in the end, I love that my friends were so supportive and embraced Justin so fully.

Of course, I still had one very important hurdle in front of me and that was introducing Justin to my kids.

Bottom line: Life goes on ... when you least expect it. And, God has a great sense of humor! As the saying goes, "If you want to see God laugh, tell Him your plans!"

INTRODUCING "FRIENDS" TO YOUR KIDS: LAYING THE PROPER FOUNDATION

*"A bend in the road is not
the end of the road...
unless you fail
to make the turn."*

~ Anonymous

As Justin and I continued to date, I realized the time was drawing near to introduce him to my kids. As important as he was becoming in my life, my kids mean the world to me, and it was important to me that they like Justin as well, and important for me to see how he did with them. If I had to make a decision between one or the other, my children would certainly win out – no argument there, and I was very transparent with Justin on this point.

I talked with people whose parents had divorced when they were kids and got all sorts of input about how to introduce Justin. I heard horror stories about things to avoid. I was never going to be the divorced woman who had a revolving door of men coming to the house to pick me up for dates. I was never going to be the woman whose kids woke up to a different man at the breakfast table every Saturday morning. I was never going to let my kids think they had to compete for my attention.

My advice for if and when you start dating is to always meet the man at a restaurant instead of having him pick you up at home. One, it's a safety thing. He doesn't have to know where you live. Two, by driving yourself, you are free to leave whenever you need or want to. Three, your kids don't have to watch you leave with a man and wonder if they are ever going to see him again, or if next weekend will bring a different man to pick you up.

I can't emphasize enough the need to present the right moral compass to your kids. I know many women who have started dating again and have had men spend the night. Then, they are "surprised" when their kids "accidentally" see the man leaving the next morning. Are you kidding me? What kind of message does that send to your children? Taking the high road means role modeling the moral compass you expect your kids to abide by.

I chose to officially introduce my kids to Justin on an afternoon that we planned to go roller skating at an indoor rink. My kids asked if they could bring a friend. I said yes, and asked if I could bring a friend as well. They said yes. It was amazing to watch my kids respond to this man who joined us skating. We all had a blast together, laughing, skating, falling and joking around. Again, it seemed like we had all been hanging out forever and that warmed my heart.

Justin invited us to join him at Buckhead Church the next morning where he was going to be singing in the children's program. I asked my kids if they wanted to go, and they immediately said yes. They thought it was pretty cool that this man they had met roller skating the day before was now singing on the stage in front of them! After church, we went out to lunch and visited the World of Coke in downtown Atlanta. I certainly had a perfect fantasy for how my kids would react to Justin. The reality was even better than the fantasy I had concocted in my head. We had a terrific day, and it was a perfect way to have my kids get to know my new "friend," and my new "friend" get to know my kids.

In the end, it was my ex- who helped me deliver a good life lesson to my kids. My son came in my room one night and said, "Daddy said Justin isn't your friend; he's your boyfriend." What a great message I was able to deliver to my son! I told him that Justin was indeed first a friend, and then later, yes, he was becoming my boyfriend. I told him in order to start loving someone, you must first like them. I told him Justin and I started as friends. And, because we were friends, I had been able to see what a great person he was, with a wonderful, generous heart, who treated me well, and who really liked my kids. I told him that as time progressed, I realized we were becoming more than just friends. I asked Harrison if he would want to have a girlfriend that he didn't like as a friend? The idea of having a girlfriend was kind of gross to him, but he completely understood the concept of liking some of the girls in his class who were "cool" and not liking some of the others who he thought were "too girly." I explained it's the same for adults. You want to be friends with someone first to see if you have the same interests and really like one another! A great lesson.

Justin and I were very cautious in front of the kids. We moved things very slowly with them. We weren't overtly physical in front of them and he certainly never stayed over, but we did let them see how a new relationship full of trust and respect looked.

When Justin proposed to me, my immediate answer was "of course, yes, I'll marry you!" We talked in infinite detail about how to share the news with my children. In the end, we sat them down on the couch and Justin began to talk. He said something to the effect of, "Kids, you know how much I love your mom, and how much I love you both. I will never be able to replace your dad, and I'm not going to try, but I do think I would be a really good step-father, and I want to spend the rest of my life with all of you. I've asked your mom to marry me. What do you think?"

The kids, bless their sweet little souls, didn't miss a beat and said, "GROUP HUG," and we all hugged one another. It was amazing, and another wonderful gift from God. As it sunk in, my daughter asked if she could be the flower girl, and my son asked if he could be "that ring guy."

Several months later, in front of a small group of family and friends, Justin and I exchanged our vows. It was perfect. The kids walked me to the spot where my Pastor and Justin were waiting, and they were an integral part of our ceremony. My brother read Jeremiah 29:11 during the ceremony because we know God truly does have a plan for each and every one of us. Justin's sister read Philippians 4:6 which says that through prayer and petition we should talk with God. How appropriate and meaningful, wouldn't you say?

I know that I would never have met Justin if I hadn't reached that point of truly forgiving my ex- and finding complete happiness with just being me. God did have a plan for my life, (and oh by the way, He certainly listened to my entire list, not simply the addendums at the end!). God knew when His timing would be right, and while I will be the first to admit God's timing was much faster than my timing would have been, who am I to argue with God, especially when He listened to my prayers so intently, and answered them so specifically.

I can't explain how it happened so quickly, and I don't try to explain it anymore. I simply accept it for what it is. Since marrying Justin, I've experienced more love, more communication, more romance, more respect, ... essentially more "marriage" than I ever have before, leading me to say on more than one occasion, "so THIS is what a great relationship is supposed to look and feel like." God does have a plan for us ... plans to give us hope and a future.

Depending on where you are at this point in your relationship with your husband or soon-to-be-ex-, with your kids, with your divorce, in the process of forgiveness, or in the process of finding peace, have faith in the fact that God does have a plan, and that you will be happy again. It may hit you when you least expect it, but life does go on.

Bottom line: Wow! God has a plan! That's clearly the bottom line on this one!

LOOKING BACK ON IT ALL:
THE EPILOGUE

"Stop every now and then.
Just stop and enjoy.
Take a deep breath.
Relax and take in
the abundance of life."

~ Anonymous

I have learned more from this experience than from any other experience in my life. I have learned more about who I am and what's important to me. I have learned about my values. I maintained my integrity. The kids are thriving. I have become stronger, yet more emotional. I have learned to love more fully and more deeply than I ever would or could have learned to do before. Our kids have benefited, my friends have benefited, our family has benefited. My faith, while always strong, has grown even stronger. My friendships, while always important, are now even more valuable. My relationships with my extended family, while always present, are now even more relevant.

Take the high road. Make sure your behaviors will make you proud in the future. Make sure you can look in the mirror. Find some humor in your situation. You can't cry all the time, even though your world is falling apart underneath you and you have no idea what your future holds. Laughter is good for you. It relieves stress. It's good for your kids, your parents, your friends, your co-workers to see you laugh! You will get through this. You will be a stronger, better woman. And you will have fabulous stories to share with your friends.

At the end of this journey, don't lose who you are, just improve who you are. It is a waste to go through a life experience like this without taking the time to learn more about who you are and becoming a better person on the other side ... otherwise, you lose. Period.

I resolved very early on in this journey that I would not go through all of this without being able to help other women who were going through a similar experience. My goal is that this book provides at least one nugget that will help you get through this. If there was even just one thought, one sentence, or one idea, that made you smarter, stronger or more strategic in dealing with your situation, then this project was a success. If I was able to bring a smile to your face in the process, then I feel ever better.

Things change. After all, change is the only constant, right? Be open to new things, be open to new experiences, be open to new relationships. Life has a really funny way of surprising you in ways you never imagined, but you have to be open to it. Don't let this experience mar you with negativity. Don't feel sorry for yourself. Don't become a cynic.

I have changed as well. People comment on it all the time. I'm more laid back now. A bit less stressed. I'm not letting anyone steal my joy. I went through hell. It felt like hell. I looked like hell. For someone to go through something like that and not learn something from it would be a waste of an experience. Take the time to reflect. How have you changed? What would you do differently next time?

My Final Bottom Line

Get your head out of the sand ∽ don't blame yourself ∽ find joy in learning new things ∽ show restraint ∽ find forgiveness ∽ practice forgiveness ∽ moderation in all things ∽ put your kids first ∽ love your family ∽ cherish your friends ∽ find a lawyer you like ∽ go see your gynecologist ∽ say thank you ∽ don't hold this inside ∽ journal and talk ∽ get rid of your stress ∽ laugh ∽ find friends you can trust ∽ find a mantra ∽ don't be in the dark on your finances ∽ always have access to the accounts ∽ stay smart ∽ be alert ∽ keep the lines of communication open ∽ use a good lawyer ∽ imitate Bruce and Demi ∽ don't be a b**** ∽ forgive selfishly ∽ forgive communally ∽ be patient with your friends ∽ keep your faith ∽ tell your mom ∽ be open to new traditions ∽ learn to show and share emotions ∽ discover what you have to learn ∽ accept change ∽ find a support group for you ∽ find a support group for your kids ∽ never badmouth your ex- in front of the kids ∽ stay calm ∽ know you will have sex again ∽ consider collaborative ∽ invite people to join you for coffee ∽ read books ∽ tell your kids together ∽ relax ∽ relish ∽ get sleep ∽ celebrate your birthday ∽ act like a kid … cry ∽ yell ∽ laugh ∽ grill out ∽ drive the boat ∽ say goodbye to your inner sailor ∽ find joy and peace ∽ go to church ∽ be open to new things ∽ make new friends ∽ continue living ∽ see a counselor ∽ talk to your minister ∽ visit your mom ∽ celebrate accomplishments ∽ talk with God ∽ lean on God ∽ make a "list" ∽ pray ∽ and pray some more ∽ and take the high road where there is always less traffic!

The End.